PRAISE FOR
WILDPRENEURS

✳   ✳   ✳

"A lot of people have dreamed about building this kind of business, and only a few of them have taken on the dream and made it work. Maybe you're a dreamer, and maybe you're a doer—and maybe, with the help of this volume, you can be both."
—BILL MCKIBBEN,
Author of *Deep Economy* and winner of the Right
Livelihood Prize, nicknamed the "alternative Nobel"

"A fascinating blend of memoir and practical advice for the entrepreneur seeking outside-the-box information on how to start your dream business. Tamara's personal stories, at times, are fabulous adventures, and at others funny, honest, and self-reflective, offering insight into her own entrepreneurial mistakes, with the hope that others can avoid them. A must read for the next Wildpreneur."
—HERTA FEELY,
Award-winning Author of *Saving Phoebe Murrow*

"I remember watching Tamara incubate her wild business idea in our college dorm. She not only dove head-first into entrepreneurship right after graduation, but she did it in the middle of the jungle with her parents. The qualities that make Tamara such a unique, resilient, and open-minded person shine through in her book with raw honesty. And she doesn't just want people to read the book and learn from her, she has intentionally curated an experience with interactive exercises so readers can develop their own blueprints. *Wildpreneurs* is inspiring and right on time for the growing movement of adventurous creatives."
—CAROLYN BARNWELL,
Media Producer at National Geographic

"Whether you're an aspiring entrepreneur looking to create the lifestyle you've always wanted, or a seasoned life-hacker looking to add a few new tricks to your trade, *Wildpreneurs* offers a practical, step-by-step roadmap full of valuable case studies and advice to help you unleash your best self. I've had the privilege to interview, learn from, and work with hundreds of free-spirited successful entrepreneurs, and many of the lessons learned I've seen time and time again are reflected in this book. I highly recommend *Wildpreneurs* for anyone looking to buck the status quo, live on their own terms, and create a passion-driven business you can be proud of."
—JEREMY JENSEN,
Creator and Host, *Adventurepreneur
Playbook Podcast*; Cofounder, Outwild

"*Wildpreneurs* is a family adventure story, a start-up guide, a real-world class in the challenges of turning passion into profit, and a call to action for dreamers—all rolled into one. Practical and inspiring."

—FRANCIS BARRY,
Contributing Editor, *Bloomberg Opinion*

"This is the kind of book business schools should use. In *Wildpreneurs*, you get all the grit; the real story and playbook, what you need to build your "wild" idea into a sustainable, thriving, hero business . . . on your own terms. We need more wild businesses like Tailwind Jungle Lodge!"

—SHARON ROWE,
CEO and Founder, Eco-Bags Products, Inc.;
Author, *The Magic of Tiny Business*

"Part action-packed toolkit, part personal manifesto for those seeking to live life on their own terms, the book is a friendly and helpful guide to anyone looking to make the jump."

—MIKE LEWIS,
Author, *When to Jump: If The Job
You Have Isn't the Life You Want*

"Tamara Jacobi approaches the age-old challenge of connecting one's life and one's livelihood with a joyful enthusiasm and an infectious sense of possibility. Equal parts how-to book, autobiography, and catalog of testimonies from dozens of comrades and role models, *Wildpreneurs* urges readers to embrace the adventure of living—and of making a living too—with passion and creativity."

—DON MITCHELL,
Author, *The Nature Notebooks*

"Living and working with heart, and focused intention, is a great prescription for a contented existence in my book, metaphorically. And it appears to be, literally, in Tamara's *Wildpreneurs* book. Designed to be picked up and set down sporadically, or for the long read with lots of breaks, this volume may not have all the answers for each reader, but there will be something for everyone in this broad view. For me, I just loved the interviews of those who have gone before and tell it like it is."

—JAN REYNOLDS,
Author, *The Glass Summit*

"This book speaks to a whole generation of unconventional thinkers—these are the people who are creating the world of our future. I feel personally connected to Tamara because she is able to accurately share what it feels like to go through the emotional ups and downs of entrepreneurship. I love all the reflection questions peppered throughout the book—it helps you immediately use what you are learning. My favorite chapter is the one on biomimicry—I love the unique entrepreneurship lessons taken from nature."

—DEREK LOUDERMILK,
Creator and Host, *The Art of Adventure Podcast*

"We don't come into the Earth, we come from it. We are as much a part of nature as a tree or an iguana. Yet, the vast majority of us are thoroughly disconnected from nature. This book is an inspirational and galvanizing call to adventure. If we are to restore and replenish our ecosystem, we must learn to love it and live within it. In this highly readable and practical book, Tamara Jacobi recounts her grand adventure and guides readers toward discovering and living their own natural purpose. This book is destined be become a classic of the genre."

—RAJ SISODIA,
Cofounder, Conscious Capitalism movement

"*Wildpreneurs* is part memoir, part blueprint for any individual looking to turn their personal dreams and passions into a viable business and craft the life they want. Jacobi's personal story of a free spirit growing up in an adventuresome family is the inspiration that allows us to hear firsthand the wisdom and experience she gleaned creating the Tailwind Jungle Lodge in the Mexican jungle. This is a book for anyone with an entrepreneurial spirit or looking for the courage to leap."

—LEE WOODRUFF,
Coauthor, *New York Times* Bestseller *In An Instant*

"At its heart, *Wildpreneurs* is a mentor for those who seek to create a path where one doesn't exist. Rife with honest experience from both her personal journey and from guest interviews, Tamara has created a guide with staying power on any bookshelf."

—COLIN BOYD,
Cofounder, Afuera Vida; Cohost, *Rewilding Parenthood Podcast*

"*Wildpreneurs* is truly a wild and creative journey for all business and lifestyle entrepreneurs! You'll find passion, inspiration, and techniques as she uses her kayaking journey to incubate her (and your!) business plans—and the Mexican land and sea is truly a supportive business partner as Tailwind Lodge takes shape. I love how Tamara thinks holistically in this book, from the usual business startup and implementation advice to tactics for self-care, work relations with others, biomimicry, and even dating while growing a business! You'll feel a sense of "tribe" by the time you finish, as Tamara

skillfully weaves a tapestry of advice from other Wildpreneurs who've already taken the plunge and provides their contact info as well! Jump in to *Wildpreneurs*, and start the adventure of growing your life and business today!"   —BEVERLY WINTERSCHEID, PH.D.,
Founding Partner, Center for Nature and Leadership

"For any dreamer wondering what is on the other side of their office window . . . Tamara Jacobi's *Wildpreneurs* is the how-to-manual, spiritual guide, and permission slip."   —NICOLE SWEDLOW,
Recipient of the Dalai Lama's
Unsung Hero of Compassion Award

"Entrepreneurs harness creativity to pursue profit and material success; adventurers dive into wilderness to connect with nature and their inner self. In *Wildpreneurs*, Tamara Jacobi celebrates her decade-long journey to braid these well-worn paths in a brand-new way, and we get to come along for the ride! Tamara and her fellow Wildpreneurs jump right into formidable challenges but learn to go slow; they plan with care and diligence but laugh heartily at their mistakes; they are ambitious with life goals but aspire every day to be "in the moment." How can a nature-loving entrepreneur resolve these potential contradictions and learn to thrive as she pursues her dreams? Dig into *Wildpreneurs* to find out!"   —JON ISHAM,
Professor of Economics and
Environmental Studies, Middlebury College

"Invoking the Zen teaching of *no mud, no lotus,* Tamara Jacobi invites readers to see how her dream of creating an ecolodge in the wilds of Mexico took shape from the stress and struggle—and exhilarating beauty—of a month-long kayaking journey through Baja. Harsh winds, wild waves, and family friction were not just challenges to overcome but the very source of the creativity and resilience that would allow her dream to come to fruition. The great gift of *Wildpreneurs* is that it gives us an inside view of the whole process, from inspiration and daydreams, through trial and error, doubt and discouragement, to the joy of fulfillment."   —JOHN BREHM,
Poet, *No Day at the Beach*

WILDPRENEURS

A PRACTICAL GUIDE TO PURSUING
YOUR PASSION AS A BUSINESS

TAMARA JACOBI

FOREWORD BY MEGAN MICHELSON

HarperCollins
Leadership

An Imprint of HarperCollins

Published by HarperCollins Leadership, an imprint of HarperCollins Focus LLC.

Book design by Aubrey Khan, Neuwirth & Associates.

ISBN 978-1-4002-1633-8 (eBook)
ISBN 978-1-4002-1632-1 (HC)

Printed in the United States of America
20 21 22 23 LSC 10 9 8 7 6 5 4 3 2 1

To my jungle family and to
free-spirited Wildpreneurs everywhere—
may a tailwind guide you wherever you dream to go.

CONTENTS

FOREWORD

It was one of the biggest storms to hit the Sierra Nevada all winter, and Tamara Jacobi had just arrived at my house near Lake Tahoe, in California. I knew Tamara from college—she was a couple of years younger than me but wise beyond her years. Mostly, I knew Tamara was always up for an adventure.

When the snow piled up outside our door and my car got buried under eight feet of snow, that didn't stop us from going skiing. "Let's just walk to the ski hill," Tamara proposed. So, we walked.

Tamara will pedal 70 miles on her road bike—long, blond braids swinging wildly from beneath her helmet—and get home in time for breakfast. She always had these eccentric, seemingly crazy ideas too. She would dream up ways to make systems more Earth-friendly and create solutions to problems in the most creative, mind-bending ways. It would not be unlike her to return from a long run and instantly go jot down notes for whatever brilliant idea popped into her head around mile 12.

All of which is it to say: I was not in the least bit surprised when Tamara told me she was opening an eco-lodge in the jungles of Mexico. "Of course you are," I responded. Tamara is not just talk. She is big ideas and total action too. When she sets her mind to something—no matter how grand or ludicrous it may seem to the rest of us—she ponders and tinkers until she sorts it out. She and her family spent years building the lodge from the ground up in a country that was not their own. She is entirely self-taught and self-motivated.

After college, instead of choosing the standard path—a career at a desk, an upward climb through our hectic, career-oriented society—Tamara went the opposite direction. She wouldn't follow any designated trail. She'd literally carve a new track for herself through the jungle.

There would be many hurdles along the way. But she would get there. When I visited her in Mexico a number of years after she opened her lodge, there was Tamara: woman of the jungle. We explored secret surf breaks and jungle trails, practiced yoga, and feasted on tacos in treetop casitas. She looked totally at home in an environment that was completely foreign to her just a few years earlier. Business was good too!

Miraculously, this process would not only make her happy, it made her successful too. That is the definition of a Wildpreneur. The real question is how do you become one? How do you take the idea that is currently a tiny, unhatched seedling in your brain and transform it into a full-fledged, money-making reality? How do you shake the cloak of anxiety and pressure to succeed that this world inevitably puts on all of us and convert that into happiness at finding a purpose that is truly your own?

You're about to find out.

This book is the story of how Tamara created a life of her own making. And how you can do that too. Listen closely to her stories—they are funny, raw, and real—and know that her advice comes from years of hard learning.

Because you can't make it to that sandy beach, with the ocean waves splashing at your feet and the sun shining down on you, without crawling through a muddy jungle first.

—Megan Michelson,
correspondent for *Outside Magazine*

INTRODUCTION

DON'T ASK WHAT THE WORLD NEEDS. ASK WHAT MAKES
YOU COME ALIVE, AND GO DO IT. BECAUSE WHAT THE
WORLD NEEDS IS PEOPLE WHO HAVE COME ALIVE.
—HOWARD THURMAN

I caught my first glimpse of the Mexican jungle in spring 2005. The ink was still fresh on the deed. It was finally official, we had just purchased five acres of tropical paradise near the charming town of San Pancho, about an hour's drive north of Puerto Vallarta. My parents and I sprinkled a shot of tequila and plunged a shovel into the highest point. I paused to inhale my new home. The jungle instantly had me under its spell; I was captivated by this wild canvas, alive with possibility.

We have been nicknamed the Swiss Family Robinson of the Mexican Pacific. Though my grandparents were indeed Swiss, I was born and raised on the Vermont/Quebec border. How did my family end up building an eco-lodge on the Mexican Pacific? Good question, I've often wondered the same. The following pages are an exploration of our journey, alongside the stories and wisdom of other intrepid free spirits—adventurepreneurs, familypreneurs, millenipreneurs, couplepreneurs, and beyond—who have blazed their own trails through life and business. We invite you to join us.

Here in the jungle, with me at the helm of our business venture, the journey to success has been WILD. After a decade of belly-flop failures and delicious triumphs, the Tailwind Jungle Lodge (eco-lodge morphed into a retreat center and adventure company) is thriving. There was no guidebook, no recipe, no model. The path was far from clear, yet somehow we managed to bushwhack our way to success—or perhaps we took the scenic route?

Prior to that first visit to the Mexican jungle in 2005, I'd been studying at Middlebury, a small liberal arts college in Vermont. I was pursuing a degree in environmental economics, a fusion created by my desire to marry the natural business worlds. In my sophomore year, I interned with a nonprofit called Natural Capitalism Solutions in Boulder, Colorado, and my junior year found me studying abroad with an ecotourism program based in Australia that opened my eyes to a variety of green building designs and permaculture possibilities.

As I stood in the jungle sprinkling tequila that day, something inside me sparked. *Had I found my purpose, my passion?* A shy voice inside my head persistently whispered *eco-lodge*. My father had often dreamed of a family business. Now I had an idea that could bring his wish to life. As I returned to academia, my vision gained momentum. When Middlebury offered a class called "Entrepreneurs 101," I was the first to claim a desk.

Yet, as I carefully composed the business plan, deliberations consumed me. *Do I really have what it takes to build a business and a life in the jungle? Is this truly what I want?* I felt as though I was teetering on the edge of a precarious cliff, reaching for a handhold. *Would I grasp the white picket fence of the modern American dream, or would I surrender to the gravitational force that was pulling my heart into the unknown?* When recruiters came to campus seeking candidates for careers in the environmental policy division of Goldman Sachs, I shoved my eco-lodge vision to the side and scheduled an interview. A steady paycheck and a more conventional job had a certain appeal. The interviewer handed me his business card and said, "Call me after graduation." Then he glanced at my flip-flops and remarked: "You know, you wouldn't be able to wear those to the office. You're sure you want to work for us?"

On a cold day in February 2007, as I skied down the Middlebury Snow Bowl in my cap and gown, I had a decision to make. In one hand, a prestigious diploma, a ticket to a traditional career. In the other hand, a freshly printed eco-lodge business plan. As I floated through the powdery snow, the tug-of-war that had lingered within me came to an abrupt halt as clarity struck. I realized that this was no longer just a business plan for my father's dream. The eco-lodge had become *my* dream—*our dream*. The jungle, my family, and Wildpreneurship beckoned. Inspiration pulled me away from Wall Street and the concrete jungle and toward the *real* jungle.

We opened for business in 2007. The Tailwind Jungle Lodge now hosts adventurers from all over the world. As a family, we have created a fun-loving and holistic business that focuses on conscious living, which includes quality of life, sustainability, and health in *all* aspects of our lives—the lodge, our community, the natural world, our relationships, our bodies, minds, and beyond.

Guests visit the Tailwind Jungle Lodge to disconnect from high-speed living, reconnect with themselves and delight in natural bliss. Adventurers come for honeymoons, weddings, family vacations, and retreats. We've even had guests from Disney and Cirque du Soleil perform acrobatics on aerial silks hung from our tropical trees. Our tree-house-style accommodations have been carefully designed to showcase and preserve the natural beauty of the jungle. My mom, fondly nicknamed "Jungle Judi," eloquently says, "We are most proud of what we haven't done here."

Life is simple. Days are filled with yoga at dawn, exploring jungle trails, and siestas on secret beaches. When the ocean is calm, we kayak. When the swell is up, we surf. The nearby town of San Pancho is vibrant and bustling, rich with local and international culture.

I have come alive in the jungle wholeheartedly—personally and professionally—a reality that is sweeter than anything I could have imagined. However, though life is relatively simple, it's far from easy—my journey through tropical living hasn't been all rainbows and butterflies. Here, the laws of nature prevail, and blood, sweat, or tears are part of the daily grind. Every moment is an adventure—some days blissful, other days brutal. Yet the mosaic of my experiences is a dream come true—a life lived to its fullest every step of the way.

Many friends and guests of the lodge have said that they've often dreamed of creating a business similar to the Tailwind Jungle Lodge. I listen, smile, and respond, "It's a good life, but there are so many things I wish I had known." So, here it is. This book is jammed with useful insights that will prepare you for the journey of Wildpreneurship: the lessons I've learned in the jungle plus tons of wisdom from others who have tuned into their wild hearts. If we can do it, you can, too.

Why "wild" entrepreneurs? We are far from conventional! As we blaze our own trails, we define success as a quality of life and richness of experience beyond dollar signs. If this book has landed in your hands, you, too, may be following an uncharted entrepreneurial road—starting your dream business, living wild, free, purposefully, out-of-the-box, tuned into your heart, and aligned with your values, whether you want to podcast from an Airstream, create an adventure company in the mountains, make organic cupcakes, open a daycare center, or become a life coach. Perhaps you're a corporate burnout, retiree, or recent graduate, the following chapters hold secrets, lessons, and practical tools to support you as you blaze your own trail from the daydreaming stage to success.

You don't necessarily have to create your own business. Being a Wildpreneur is about living consciously and designing your life path. My hope is that my experiences alongside the wisdom of my fellow Wildpreneurs will ignite your courage, empower you to explore your dreams, and launch you into the greatest adventure of your life.

The journey begins now! It won't always be easy, but we're here to support you through the potholes and celebrate the summits. We are delighted to invite you to become part of our jungle family. Wherever you are, as you turn the pages of *Wildpreneurs* and take action in your own life—personally and professionally—you will be joining a tribe of free-spirited Wildpreneurs. United, we can turn our individual ripples of inspiration into waves of positive change that will spread the love of wild and holistic businesses globally.

For support throughout your journey (downloadable pdfs, guided audio exercises, resources, and more), check out wildpreneurs.com /resources. Watch for the ♥ symbol—this indicates supplemental materials available online. Visit us in the jungle at tailwindjunglelodge.com.

Tailwind Jungle Lodge Timeline

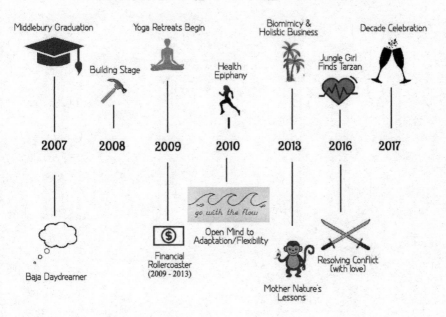

Middlebury Graduation

Yoga Retreats Begin

Biomimicy & Holistic Business

Decade Celebration

Building Stage

Health Epiphany

Jungle Girl Finds Tarzan

2007　2008　2009　2010　2013　2016　2017

Baja Daydreamer

Financial Rollercoaster (2009 - 2013)

go with the flow

Open Mind to Adaptation/Flexibility

Mother Nature's Lessons

Resolving Conflict (with love)

CHAPTER ONE

BAJA
DAYDREAMER

A JOURNEY OF A THOUSAND MILES
BEGINS WITH A SINGLE STEP. —LAOZI[1]

My journey as a Wildpreneur began in the Sea of Cortez on March 3, 2007, right after my graduation ceremony at Middlebury. Fierce winds gusted more than 70 miles an hour as my father, Tigre, my brother, Rhett, and I anxiously prepared to launch our fully loaded expedition kayaks. This family adventure would be a celebration of Tigre's sixtieth birthday and my college graduation—a two-month journey through the pristine beauty of raw wilderness with dazzling white sand, azure water, and a ceiling of stars like diamonds. Our goal? To paddle more than 800 miles, from the sparse village of San Felipe to Baja's capital city of La Paz, in search of paradise. Yet, as I pondered the flurry of angry waves and the alluring yet dauntingly wild coastline, I was frozen with trepidation. Were we embarking on an impossible journey? My inner voice trilled in alarm. What was I getting myself into? I took a deep breath, stretched my arms up to the sky in a superhero power pose, and we ventured into the unknown. Let's do this, I resolved. If the wind howls, I will howl back. No risk, no reward.

WILDPRENEUR
TRAIL MAP—CHAPTER 1

This chapter launches us into the transformative process of making a dream come to life. Be warned! Anything is possible and adventure awaits around each bend—intense challenge and deliciously profound reward awaits:

- Get a taste of wild living and an overview of the fundamental qualities and values that define Wildpreneurship.
- Learn the practical steps to get you started with the daydreamer phase of Wildpreneurship.

Plan to take time for this crucial stage. Our vision for the Tailwind Jungle Lodge germinated and sprouted in the Baja wilderness well before it blossomed in the jungle.

✻   ✻   ✻

PAINFUL BEGINNINGS

I had barely enough time to disrobe from my Middlebury College graduation gown and ditch my ski boots before grabbing my flip flops and heading to the Baja. Miraculously, we'd managed to fit all our tropical gear and supplies into a 23-foot tandem kayak for my father and me, and a 17-foot kayak for Rhett. My freshly printed business plan was safely tucked away in my boat and my mind.

As we set out on that first morning, facing merciless winds of up to 70 miles an hour, I gripped my paddle with white knuckles. After traveling only two miles down the coastline, my muscles and mind ached with tension. Frustrated, miserable, and defeated, we precariously landed to make camp at a deserted construction zone. We had to dodge rusty nails as we desperately sought shelter from the raging wind and blowing sand that ripped at my skin. Any romantic notions I'd had of the journey were snatched away by harsh reality. Ugh . . . paradise? I think not. I definitely won't be needing my teenie-weenie polka-dot bikini!

Our plan had been to cover at least 20 miles each day. At this pace, that would be an impossibility, yet steady progress was crucial in order for us to reach our resupply points for fresh drinking water and food. *How would we survive nearly two months of this?* I felt like a tiny, floundering fish in a vast, ominous sea.

After twenty-four interminable hours, the wind suddenly evaporated. Giddy with relief, we relaunched our kayaks into a sea of mercury-colored water and majestic stillness. A fishing boat cruised by us, waved, and bolstered our spirits as they congratulated us on making it through our first El Norte—an infamous Baja windstorm that typically lasts for three days—a wind that would be forever imprinted in our minds. "No mud, no lotus," says Buddhist monk Thích Nhất Hạnh. I would soon discover that this is a key mantra for Wildpreneurs.

Yet, even on calmer waters, I struggled. My body ached from the rigorous paddling regime, and my restless monkey mind battled severe anxiety from long hours of being confined to the boat. By the time we made camp each night, I was ready to snap my paddle over my knee and burn it as kindling. But the sound of El Tigre's happy whistle as he collected firewood and cast the fishing rod pierced my heart. His bleached blonde hair glowed golden in the dusk light, his skin bronzed and weathered handsomely, there was a joyful sparkle in his ageless green eyes. He was clearly thriving—at home in the wild, alive with the thrill of his birthday journey, and excited about whatever might await us down the coast. I resolved that there would be no quitting; I couldn't let El Tigre down. I would overcome my weaknesses and get tough. *I am whole-heartedly committed to this adventure.*

You will inevitably confront challenge and discomfort as you begin blazing your trail through wild business. Things won't always be what you expected, so be prepared. As we go boldly forward, we must believe in ourselves and get tough (emotionally and physically). Dig deep—you have what it takes. The winds will blow, but a delicious calm will follow.

MASTER OF ADVENTURE

It had come as no surprise when my father invited my brother and me to join him on the Baja. El Tigre is a man known for his sense of adventure. He'd earned the nickname "Tiger" at just six months old. My grandmother often kept him on a leash (yes, a real leash!), fearful that his relentless curiosity would tempt him into danger. My father had grown up between Manhasset, New York, and his parents' cottage on Lake Memphremagog—a charming lake that straddles Quebec and Vermont. Post high school, my father was lured by the call of the wild and followed his heart to the mountains and the waves, from Alaska to California, inevitably drifting south to Mexico in the sixties. It wasn't long before he was surfing the idyllic waves of the "Mexican Malibu" at Punta de Mita, just north of Puerto Vallarta, where his name became "El Tigre." Life as a family man didn't slow his adventurous spirit—he simply brought my mom, my brother, and me along with him into the wilderness.

STRENGTH AND ENDURANCE

The Baja had broken me. A week into our trip, I hit bottom (tears gushed . . . oh, yes), which luckily seemed to trigger a miraculous transformation—as though the natural extremes had torn me apart in order to rebuild a new, stronger, better me.

We launched our kayaks onto a rosy sea, illuminated by the radiant glow of dawn. We glided through the kaleidoscopic stillness; our paddles dipped exquisitely synchronized, arms strengthened from continual paddling. I gratefully welcomed this endurance and newfound energy. The stillness of the water that morning reflected an unusual calm in my mind; blissful presence, wonder, and awe had come to my rescue. In the days that followed, we found the paradise we had sought. From oasis islands and mysterious caves to secret hot springs. As sunlight faded to moonlight, we surrendered to the raw beauty of Mother Nature.

And then the dreaded El Norte returned. This time, we knew what to expect and smartly stayed ashore. As the wind howled, we gritted our sandy teeth, and hunkered down behind a patch of boulders. Survival instincts kicked in as we carefully rationed our fresh water in fear that we wouldn't make it to our next resupply point in time. Three days later, bliss returned and we gratefully paddled to a tiny fishing village. Fresh water had never tasted so sweet. There will be highs and there will be lows; it's a wild ride. No mud, no lotus, indeed.

EL TIGRE, COFOUNDER OF THE TAILWIND JUNGLE LODGE

Builder, designer, master daydreamer.
"I've never been one for the status quo."

What was your inspiration for starting a family business?
I have always wanted to do something with my family, evidenced by the way they were brought up (see family stories in chapter 8). I realized that, once my kids grew up, they would sprout wings and fly away. So, what better than a family business to keep us together?

What has allowed our family business to thrive?
Patience. And with time, everyone has pretty much figured out what their strong points are and how they can be integrated into the business. We all occasionally have disagreements, but ultimately those challenge us and make us try harder to be more understanding and therefore a stronger business. Oh, and selective hearing . . . hah!

What does your ideal day in the jungle look like?
Sunny, cloudless, no wind, and a nice ocean swell. First, a wake-up walk in the jungle with Poncho (our yellow lab), fix a few things around the lodge, then off to the ocean for either kayaking or SUP (stand-up paddleboard). Then some yoga and stretching, followed by a cold beer in the shade of a palm tree. Siesta, sunset, fresh tuna on the grill, and a cold margarita in hand, hanging with my family, friends, or guests at the lodge. Perfect day!

What advice would you give to someone considering starting a wild business?
To go as slowly as you can afford to. Become involved in the community so you can gain people's trust. Be friendly and engaging with all your guests/clients/customers, no matter how hard it might be at times.

What is your favorite aspect of being a Wildpreneur?
The freedom of waking up every day and knowing that it is my day to do whatever I wish. No schedule (at least, not many). I also love interacting with all of the wonderful people we have hosted at the lodge over the years.

Anything else you'd like to share?
I'm grateful to my family! Whether it be hauling stones or mopping floors, it's a team effort.

✳   ✳   ✳

SLOW

The Baja gave us the gift of time, and plenty of it—a reprieve from the speedy modern world from which we had come. Had we been paddling for minutes or hours? Did it matter? The endless seconds were only interrupted by the sounds of the wind, waves, birds, and occasional visits from jumping manta rays, sea lions, whales, and other curious creatures who accompanied us along the way.

3-D GLASSES

Attuned to the basics of survival, life became relatively simple. As we settled into our paddling rhythm, my arms moved mechanically—programmed by repetition—which set my mind free to wander. I lost myself in the peaceful dance of the water currents and ripples. When my thoughts drifted to the business plan I'd safely tucked away, jolts of inspiration reminded me of my jungle lodge dream.

Yet, simultaneously, I felt a strange hesitation. *Daydreaming is wrong,* nagged my inner voice. Was that guilt I was feeling? My pragmatic, type A predisposition had been exacerbated by years of rigorous academia that admonished daydreaming as a childish impediment to productivity. Life with El Tigre—a chronic daydreamer who'd bounced from one crazy adventure idea to the next—had also made me skeptical and intolerant of those with their head in the clouds. Consequently, I had adopted diametrically opposed behavior, a laser-like focus that earned me the nickname "Turbo Tam" in college.

Thus, when I'd graduated with a business plan in hand, I had been ready to charge forward at full speed toward my target. I'd actually perceived this Baja birthday expedition as a burden, my duty as a daughter. Days of doing nothing but propelling a kayak south had seemed mindless and unproductive—like slamming on the brakes of my mission. *We'd already purchased the land in the jungle, I'd written the business plan, why wait? Couldn't we just get on with it already?*

Now, as we paddled through the middle of nowhere, my perception had shifted. *This is an opportunity to see where my daydreams take me.* I had already typed a practical road map to guide my dream, but now, as I flourished in the freedom and excitement of the wilds, that business plan seemed dry, boring, and constrained; focused on dollar signs and conventional business strategies that didn't suit us. It was time to put on the 3-D glasses and get a little wild. *Could the wild rhythm and natural simplicity we'd found in the Baja be applied to business?* It was prime time for daydreamin' with El Tigre—the dream master—at the helm.

DAYDREAMER

I unleashed my mind, opened to vast possibilities, and took my first *real* steps toward becoming a Wildpreneur. "Logic will get you from A to B. Imagination will take you everywhere," says Einstein. With each mile of coastline, my eco-lodge dream morphed as I infused my creativity, personality, and inspiration into the preexisting plan (my parents would be partners in the business, but they entrusted me with creating the shape and plan for the lodge). I daydreamed of what we might build: hanging bridges, tree houses, pulley systems, bamboo huts, palapas, yurts, wooden decks, rocking chairs, and hammocks. I imagined a bar that served all-you-can-eat tacos, green smoothies and bottomless margaritas. I fantasized about candlelight dinners for two on a jungle rooftop under a full moon. I envisioned teaching my guests to surf; I could hear their giggles of delight as they rode their first waves. El Tigre chimed in, "Don't forget kayaking tours, too!"

I eagerly rode the flood of ideas and envisioned my dream life. Good thing that dreamin' doesn't cost much, or it would have left me in debt for life. In those Baja moments, I felt rich, alive, wild, and free. No limits, nothing but endless potential. Many great achievements have started as dreams—the oak sleeps in the acorn.

GET STARTED:
SET YOUR DAYDREAMS FREE

If you were told as a kid to get your head out of the clouds, it's time to rewire that thinking. Why is it that daydreamers have gotten a bad rap, while visionaries are celebrated? Visionaries like Yvon Chouinard (Patagonia founder) or Steve Jobs (Apple cofounder) were daydreamers long before they took action. Einstein was a classic daydreamer, yet consider all that he achieved! Daydreaming is an essential prerequisite to action. Wildpreneurship starts here. Pause, surrender to your daydreams, and see where they take you. Be realistic (we are all beholden to the laws of gravity), but don't hold back.

LAUNCH YOUR DAYDREAMS ♥

Set yourself a timer for 10 or 15 minutes, or longer, and answer the following questions. (Even if the answers don't come right away, keep sitting until the timer dings. You never know what ideas might pop up.) Let your thoughts flow abstractly, draw a tree diagram, or whatever approach works best for you.

- What is my ideal lifestyle? What life do I crave?
- Why do I want to live this way?
- How can I design my dream business to suit that ideal lifestyle? Or how might I adjust my lifestyle to suit my dream business? Are my dream life and dream business compatible?
- Where do I want to live, work, and play?
- Do I want to be a Wildpreneur? Should I be a Wildpreneur? Does this suit my personality or ideal lifestyle?
- When will I get started?
- What would today look like if I was following my dream? What would next month look like? Next year?
- Will this create positive change in my life, my community, and the world around me?

Special tip: If your home life is busy and time for daydreaming is scarce, schedule yourself a personal retreat or a wilderness adventure. The natural world is kindling that will ignite your daydreams.

✳ ✳ ✳

TURBULENCE

Even daydreams can hit speed bumps. Tension soared in our tandem kayak when El Tigre and I debated the use of technology in our wild business venture. My father saw no use for the internet, cell phones, or other devices in our eco-lodge endeavor. As a millennial, I fervently believed otherwise. My travels had opened my eyes to the usefulness of the internet for travelers and hosts. There had been a shift—travel guides were still being used, but travelers were now researching their accommodations and making reservations online prior to arrival. This was a foreign concept to El Tigre, who'd always favored a more spontaneous approach to travel. Sometimes you just can't teach an old tiger new tricks.

When our debates intensified and steam started coming out of my ears, I willed my paddle to morph into a sword, ready to attack. In these moments, El Tigre joked that my "grouch-o-meter was getting a high rating," which only fueled my irritation. However, instead of turning into a weapon, my loyal paddle simply propelled me through my discomfort, keeping me steady until we reached calmer waters. Only years later would I understand my paddle's wisdom as I learned to work through conflict from a place of love. The ability to persevere through discomfort and find calm amid turmoil and conflict (in many forms) is invaluable for Wildpreneurs.

DEVIL'S ADVOCATE

Rhett poked at my daydreams with questions as he paddled effort-lessly alongside us in his banana-colored kayak. At nineteen years old, Rhett had taken a semester off from the University of Vermont to join this expedition. Rhett's surfer physique and blonde beach bum looks paired with his contagious passion for life, curiosity, and delight at simple pleasures make him well loved. Rhett and I had spent most of our childhood sharing a tent as we journeyed through the wilderness with our parents. Consequently, Rhett knows me better than anyone. We'd biked 2,000 miles of the Continental Divide National Scenic Trail, backpacked Vermont's 270-mile Long Trail and California's 220-mile John Muir Trail, and mountaineered the Pico de Orizaba (at 18,490 feet, it's the third highest peak in North America). This Baja expedition was yet another link in the web of experiences we'd share as siblings and true friends.

As we paddled together, Rhett naturally assumed the role of devil's advocate. I initially greeted his prodding and keen commentary with hostility. *Why should I listen to my little brother?* The answer came loud and clear: *Because I've got nothing to lose; his insights could be valuable.* Swallow your ego.

"Who would be your ideal client/guest?" Rhett inquired.

"Adventurers," I responded without hesitation.

"What kind of adventurers?" he prodded.

"Hmm . . . I think solo travelers or couples looking for a wild and unique natural experience. Families, too; kids will love the jungle."

"OK, but I don't think grandma would be thrilled to climb up a ladder to a tree house." he chuckled.

"Good point. Maybe we should build a variety of different styles for our guest accommodations. The bungalows will be more tree-house style, then we can build some fancier casitas closer to the parking area so they're easy to access. Grandma would like that," I replied.

Rhett plowed in to his next inquisition. "How will you get your first guests to come? Nobody knows about the lodge."

"Well, I definitely need to get a website going, but I can't do much until I have some photos of our bungalows. To get the ball rolling, I plan to send an email out to everyone I know—friends, family, and your friends, too—hopefully I'll get some feedback and someone will volunteer to be our first guests."

"Guinea pigs! Poor them," Rhett said, smirking.

And so went our banter. *What about food? What would I charge? What would make the lodge unique?* Questions and answers shot through my head like arrows. Some hit the target, others missed by a mile. Bull's-eyes were collected and safeguarded in my mind.

A DEVIL'S ADVOCATE RUDE Q&A ♥

When you're floating around in dreamland, you may not want to hear questions that contradict your concept. But that's actually *exactly* what you need—a devil's advocate to challenge your assumptions. Your peers and fellow Wildpreneurs offer tremendous feedback, and they're excellent sounding boards. Criticism can hurt, but it gets easier with practice and it will ultimately make you and your business stronger!

I recommend asking for criticism before it shows up unexpectedly. Try inviting your most analytical and direct amigos over for dinner and set them loose on your idea. Be sure to wear your thickest skin—be ready for the challenge. Have them ask you questions such as the following:

- Who is your ideal customer?
- Why are you the best person to create this business?
- Your biggest competitors just dropped their price to $0. How do you continue to justify your price point?
- If the economy declines, how will you survive?

Use your devil's advocate to clarify your marketing messages, identify your target customer profile, establish what will set you apart from the competition, and more.

✹   ✹   ✹

SURVIVAL THROUGH TRIAL AND ERROR

As the extreme wilderness steadily tested us mind and body, each day was a journey all on its own—from dawn to dusk, natural simplicity was laced with challenge and reward. Though days collectively added up to steady progress toward our southern goal, obstacles awaited around every bend. We paddled through ominous waves, finally pulling our boats up onto a beach, only to be greeted by an army of flying bugs on shore, which drove us back out onto the water and wind in search of respite. I awoke to relieve myself one night and serendipitously glanced up to see our boats floating away in the extreme high tide—the ocean gods conspiring to leave us stranded.

Through trial and error, we gradually learned the ways of the Baja wilds—wind, waves, tides, swells, peninsulas, wildlife, heat, cold, and other forces continually at play. We learned to savor, ration, and conserve every drop of the little fresh water we were able to carry between resupply points. Together we adapted and found balance, strategy, perseverance, and unity. The unpredictable extremes of the wilderness were mitigated by our strength and stability as a team—as a family. Learning how to navigate the turbulent waters and wilds of the Baja enabled us to cultivate the fundamental qualities that would prepare us for the challenge of Wildpreneurship: patience, strength, courage, support, and much experience living outside our comfort zones.

BAJA MANTRAS
FOR WILDPRENEURS

The Baja had much to teach us—paddling would be only one aspect of the daily ordeal. The following elements of our Baja routine are simple yet essential mantras for Wildpreneurs:

1. There is always time to **pause and savor the natural display.** As we relaunched our boats each morning, we marveled at the sun's first rays as they spilled over the horizon.
2. **No mud, no lotus.** There will be winds, but a blissful calm will follow.
3. **Do the work, make progress, be efficient.** Find a routine and rhythm that work for you.
4. **Set yourself goals, but be flexible and go with the flow. You never know what awaits just around the bend.** Our progress depended on tides, winds, currents, and the power of our arms. Should we camp on this beach? What if paradise is just around the corner? Our maps were little help—all beaches look the same on a topo.
5. **Learn from nature.** Dolphins, whales, sea lions, pelicans, and other wildlife had much to teach.
6. **Play and explore.** We camped on beaches of pink pebbles, giant shells, whale bones, and sand like powdered sugar; by ship wrecks, deserted eco-lodges, cement mines, and mafia mansions. Once the relentless sun had fallen lower in the sky, El Tigre would announce, "I'm going to wander the beach in search of I don't know what and I don't care." He would return grinning, pockets overflowing with exquisite shells—"treasure!" he proclaimed.
7. **Self-care.** Though we journeyed together, we took much needed alone time for yoga, siesta, and so on.

8. **Eat for energy and health.** If you're running on an empty tank, you're not going anywhere.
9. **Recharge your batteries.** When the stars came out, we collapsed into our tents. Sleep!
10. **Leave no trace.** We left every beach exactly as we found it.

✳   ✳   ✳

CELEBRATING EL TIGRE

On March 18, El Tigre turned sixty. A month on the Baja had allowed me to see my father in fresh light. Where I had once felt impatience with his daydreams, I now felt gratitude and a genuine appreciation for his free spirit. I also realized how instrumental his dreams had been in the evolution of my own life and dreams, even though we had often clashed on the details. El Tigre embodied the essence of Wildpreneurship and had passed that along to me.

Many of his daydreams had never come to fruition; they'd simply drifted off, back to the mysterious place that ideas come from. However, some dreams, such as the Baja adventure, had become a reality well worth waiting for. The daydreaming period had been a litmus test of a dream's resilience. Perhaps the daydreams that persist through the rigors of reality are the ones that are truly worth pursuing?

El Tigre's intrigue with the Baja had begun when he'd first explored it on a surfing trip in the sixties. It wasn't until decades later—at a tiny cabin where we'd stopped to rest on the final day of adventure backpacking Vermont's Long Trail—that he'd picked up a paddling magazine and read an article about kayaking the Baja. He knew then that it was a trip he *must* do.

He started saving his pennies—an essential ingredient for any wild pursuit. It wouldn't take much; he'd always had a knack for living and traveling on a shoestring budget. This philosophy was further facilitated by his passion for simplicity and minimalism. "More stuff means more problems; just keep it simple," is one of his favorite mantras. As he gathered funds, he created his plan—spending hours studying maps, books, and magazines as he researched the journey ahead. When he had just enough money to budget for gear, supplies, and travel, he invited my brother and me to join him, and we set a date together. It was time to turn his Baja dream into a reality.

We celebrated El Tigre's birthday with Cuba libres by the fire. As the rum dwindled in the bottle, we plunged into a collective eco-lodge daydream. El Tigre doodled building designs in the sand by the fire, while I watched the reflection of the flames dance happily in his eyes.

SELF-DOUBT AND FEAR

As we continued southward, self-doubt arrived to sabotage my daydreams. *Do I have what it takes to be an entrepreneur? What if I fail?* As you consider your own wildpreneur path, I'm sure that these questions have nagged you as well. My only job had been a brief stint as a ski instructor in Vermont, a giant leap from creating a business in the Mexican jungle. Seeing my drooped shoulders, my dad grabbed my salty pigtails, looked me hard in the eye, and said, "You *know* you have what it takes. Surely, our adventures as a family have taught you that if you dig deep, get tough, and believe that you will succeed, you *will* succeed, *and* no matter what direction it takes you, it will be a valuable life experience! Let the strength and confidence that you've shown here on the Baja set the tone for your future endeavors." Indeed, my parents had taught me to live life without limits—no room for self-doubt. My parents had always been my personal cheerleading squad, imprinting the mantra "believe in yourself" into my psyche.

"What about fear?" I'd challenged the boys. We'd all become acquainted with this emotion in the past few weeks. Fear was clearly a valuable survival instinct that often guided our decisions in this wild place. If a camp spot felt unsafe, we would move on, if the ocean was too rough, we would not paddle. We mutually agreed that fear is healthy and necessary, but should be consistently dissected, considered, and never perceived as a barrier or excuse. Though fear may slow progress, it also prompts a clear evaluation of a situation, a valuable opportunity to analyze and choose your path.

Fear is a universal experience. Even the smallest insect feels it. We wade in the tidal pools and put our finger near the soft open bodies of sea anemones and they close up. It's part of being alive. Fear is a natural reaction to moving closer to the truth.

—PEMA CHÖDRÖN[2]

Shortly after El Tigre's birthday, I resolved to use fear as a friend. Our eco-lodge project, just like our Baja adventure, would undoubtedly be heavy with challenge. Fear would keep me alert and prepared. I would use it as my prompt to analyze a situation, breathe, and assess. Neither fear nor self-doubt would stand in my way.

The next time you encounter fear, meet it head on. Deconstruct your fear—tap into its wisdom, channel it, use fear to your advantage. You must also be resistant to the fear of others. Wildpreneur Shanti Tilling, founder of SweatPlayLive, explains, "You have to just follow your heart and go for it! There are going to be plenty of people around you that cannot see outside of their box or cubicle. You might hear advice or get resistance from people living with a fear-based mindset. Do not let them squash your dream."

Let go of the mentality of fear. Instead, fill your head with positive self-talk and surround yourself with encouragement and support—people who believe in you—your friends, family, or coach. You are at the beginning of a *very* long journey, and support is an essential ingredient. Find the people who pick you up, dust you off, give you courage to confront fear and keep you on track (we may also learn from those who haven't confronted their fears and have regrets).

JORDAN DUVALL, IGNITE YOUR SOUL BRAND

Brand strategy and support for spiritual entrepreneurs.
"This is the work I was born to do. It is my gift and my passion."

What advice would you give to a potential Wildpreneur?
Commit 100 percent and *decide* your success is inevitable.
Draw on your grit and resourcefulness, because you will need
them. Stop defining yourself by your failures and start learning
from them. Get a mentor. Set boundaries. Lead with love.

What do you wish you'd known prior to getting started?
Success is a long game. You have to have the stamina and be
in it for reasons that are deeper than money.

✳   ✳   ✳

PASSION, PURPOSE, TALENT?

As my confidence grew, another deliberation chimed into my inner
dialogue: *Is this my passion, my calling?* As with the Baja journey,
once I was committed, there would be no quitting. Now was the time
to evaluate my true desires.

What is passion anyhow? It's defined as a powerful (sometimes
uncontrollable) emotion that is a confluence of interest and purpose.
Did I have interest? Definitely. My jungle-lodge vision had been tug-
ging at my sleeve for many years, a perfect melding of my degree in
environmental economics.

Purpose? Absolutely. It had been love at first sight of the jungle—
my heart had called me to preserve, share, and create a sustainable
family business.

What about talent? Is talent a prerequisite to passion? I chewed on this. Did I have a natural talent for running an eco-lodge? Maybe. A knack for wild living? Definitely. But a talent for hospitality? I had no experience (though my great-grandmother had been an innkeeper, and I hoped I'd inherited that gene). What I *did* know for sure was that I was resolutely prepared to work hard, learn, and cultivate the skills that I needed. Talent is always helpful, but if you don't have natural talent and are determined, you can develop the skills you need—the U.S. Census shows that approximately 50 percent of entrepreneurs don't have a formal college degree.[3] There are many different approaches to thinking, creating, and playing the game of life. "Passion isn't about credentials, it's about commitment," says Marianne Williamson.[4]

With these considerations, my qualms were appeased. *This is the work I truly want to do. This is how I will make a positive impact. I will regret it if I don't try.* With this, I found a deep sense of clarity and sense of peace. However, this feeling may not be the same for you or other Wildpreneurs. For some, passion strikes as a lightning bolt. For others, it takes years to germinate and flourish.

What is your passion? Or if "passion" isn't your descriptive word of choice, try using "excitement" as a barometer. "Listen to your sympathetic nervous system—what gives you the itch?" asks podcaster Tim Ferriss.[5] Explore these questions as you consider your interplay of excitement, passion, purpose, and talent.

EVALUATE YOUR PASSION, PURPOSE, TALENT ♥

Set your timer once again (10 or 15 minutes) and ask yourself the following:

- Is this my passion or my purpose?
- What do I truly want to achieve in my life?

- What excites and inspires me? Where do I feel motivated? What makes me jump out of bed in the morning?
- What makes me come alive?
- What am I likely to stick with? Is this just a fleeting idea or a project I could commit to? (This may be hard to know until you try it, but it's worth pondering the question now anyhow.)
- Do I have natural talent? Do I need talent to chase my dream?
- What would I do with my life if money were no object? What is my purpose? My calling?
- If I work in my passion, will I still love it? (Some say that work eventually squelches passion.) Is it better to keep my passion as a hobby and pursue a different project as a career?
- What are the potential risks and rewards of following my passion?
- If I have multiple passions, which one might I want to focus my business on? Or can I incorporate them all into my business?

BIG QUESTION: Will I regret it if I don't give this wild idea a try?

✳   ✳   ✳

SIMPLICITY

Near the end of our journey, on a rare lazy Baja afternoon, I fished my business plan out of my dry bag. This original plan had proposed taking on investors and building the lodge quickly. This approach would mean significant debt, ideally followed by a quick return with high risk.

El Tigre plopped himself down on the sand beside me. He studied the crumpled pages for a moment and suggested: "Why don't we start small and keep it simple? Less stress. We can move forward slowly and steadily, grow as we can afford it. Let's focus our energy and keep from spreading ourselves too thin."

Seduced by the simplicity of the Baja, El Tigre's philosophy now resonated with me. Why overcomplicate things? With that, I molded a new plan that focused on smart simplicity, quality above quantity, and a philosophy of slow and steady. Particularly if this is your first entrepreneurial pursuit, test the waters with a simple plan—not a lazy plan, a smart plan (there is a big difference!). Flex your entrepreneurial muscle, see how it feels with less pressure and lower financial risk. As you build momentum, you can always add on more. This wisdom is evident in all of Mother Nature's grandest creations and designs—the biggest trees start out as tiny seeds.

VISUALIZE

As we approached our final destination (La Paz) I reigned in my abstract daydreams and visualized myself in action getting the lodge started. I pictured my return to the jungle. I envisioned myself working alongside El Tigre and my mom (now fondly nicknamed "Jungle Judi") as we brought the lodge to life, one plank and hammer swing at a time. I visualized the big picture and the little details; I could see us decorating the bungalows with shells, candles, and tropical blossoms. I saw myself excitedly greeting our first guests.

My dear friend and lifelong Wildpreneur Shannon Hughes attributes the power of intention and manifestation to his success. "It took me many years to truly believe that I can do anything I set my mind to. Manifesting is real, and learning how to have clear vision and act upon it is an art form," says Hughes.

Visualize your dream coming true. See yourself in action, set your intention. Visualization is one of the secrets to success. Start this habit now—either on your own or try a guided visualization exercise. ♥

SET YOUR INTENTION— DAILY VISUALIZATION PRACTICE

Take a moment at the beginning and end of each day to pause, reflect, and visualize:

MORNING RITUAL

What am I excited about today? (Envision your day, set a positive intention)

What might throw me off? (Can you predict the speed bumps?)

How can I move through these challenges as my best self? (Visualize yourself flowing through your day on track with your goals.)

EVENING RITUAL

What did I enjoy today?

Was I my best self today? What could I have done differently?

Inspiration Source:
High Performance Habits by Brendon Burchard

✳   ✳   ✳

TAILWIND

Our final Baja moments found us nibbling on our last stores of dried food. The guys drooled as they chattered about steak and cold beer. I heard myself say, "Though I definitely won't miss beans, rice, and oatmeal, I will be sad to see this journey come to an end."

The journey added up to 49 days, 47 campfires, more than 800 miles and millions of paddle strokes. Nearly two months in the Baja wilds had fueled my inspiration while strengthening, preparing, and empowering me to become a Wildpreneur. I'd discovered that with the pains, challenges, and risk of adventure comes vast reward. In fact, the difficulties and misadventure we'd encountered along the way had actually been part of the richness of the experience.

As we paddled the final strokes into the harbor of La Paz, we savored the gentle wind at our backs. Thus, the name "Tailwind" Jungle Lodge was born. We'd been irrevocably convinced that life is much better when you have a supportive wind at your back. As we paddled our final miles, tears of elation, relief, exhaustion, sadness, and happiness streaked my freckled cheeks.

On April 19, we proudly boarded the La Paz ferry, relishing our success. As we lugged our kayaks up the ramp, fellow passengers gawked. We looked as though we'd been lost at sea—our clothing tattered, torn, and faded by the sun and salt. The guys' beards were unruly, my braids were matted into snarls, and my dark eyebrows bleached white. Once on deck, we gorged ourselves on fresh tacos and sipped Bloody Marys. El Tigre raised his class and declared, "Now *that* was an adventure."

As the ferry pulled out of the port and carried us east toward the Mexican mainland, I whispered a final prayer of gratitude to the Baja. I savored the deliciousness of the moment—I felt as though I had just ridden one of the biggest, scariest, and most exciting waves of my life. Now I was floating between sets, grateful for the calm, but filled with anticipation. Mom and Poncho, our yellow lab, awaited us in Mazatlán, eager to shuttle us home to the jungle. What would the next wave—our jungle lodge adventure—bring? Would I ride it gracefully?

Or would it push me under? As the mainland of the Mexican Pacific coast appeared on the horizon, I wondered what life as a wildpreneur might have in store.

VITINA BLUMENTHAL, WANDERFULSOUL

Motto: Self-discovery retreats globally.

"A perfect day has its beautiful imperfections. That's what makes it so perfect. The same applies to life as a Wildpreneur!"

What was your inspiration to create WanderfulSoul?

I worked in the fashion, music, and entertainment industry for five years and ended up completely stressed and burnt out. I was working eighty-plus hours a week and hardly getting any sleep. I had a breaking point after yelling at a poor taxi driver when heading to an event. I got out of the cab and felt like I had completely lost myself.

I fled to India to do my first yoga teacher training. On the final day of training, my teacher, Raviji, said to me: "Vitina, you are so relaxed. When you first got here, I was scared of you."

I responded, "What do you mean you were scared of me?!"

He went on to explain that the pace of my voice had been going a million miles a minute. That was when I realized how much I had slowed down, and I felt so connected to myself. I knew I wasn't the only one who felt burnt out, stressed, anxious, and completely disconnected. It was that moment I knew I wanted to take people on life-changing experiences around the world.

What do you wish you'd known prior to getting started?

Trust and train your intuition. It might result in a few "mistakes," but for the long haul it will be your best asset.

Also, having quality guidance from someone who has been successful at building a business is key. That said, there is a cap on how many mentors you look to for guidance—too many cooks in the kitchen can be confusing.

What's your favorite part about being a Wildpreneur?
The sense of freedom. I've strategically built all my businesses so I can be mobile and flexible. The thought of being able to book a plane ticket whenever I want truly invigorates me. I also love that I get to connect with like-minded people who equally share a passion for what they do. We feed off one another's ideas and energy, and they're a huge source of support.

* * *

ADELANTE!

As you surrender to the current of your daydreams and desires, be patient. Let your ideas germinate and sprout. Tune into your inspiration. Where will the wind blow you? What uniquely beautiful footprints will you leave on this Earth?

CHAPTER TWO

GET DIRTY & CREATE

THE WAY TO GET STARTED IS TO QUIT
TALKING AND BEGIN DOING. —WALT DISNEY

WILDPRENEUR
TRAIL MAP #2 ♥

Let's roll up our sleeves and get tough. This chapter will guide you through the initial creation stage of your wild business. You'll:

- Make a clear plan (and a backup plan).
- Consider the nuts and bolts of your business design.
- Establish a routine and make steady progress.
- Test your product/service and attract your first clients.
- Become a master of artful mistake making.
- Find your grit: Persistence is the only way forward.

✶   ✶   ✶

JUNGLE BEGINNINGS

Fresh off the Baja, we returned to the jungle in April 2007. It was time to move from "wantrepreneur" status to digging into the hard work of turning our daydreams into reality. Summon your focus, strength, and determination as you give this challenging phase everything you've got (you don't want to look back and wish that you'd tried harder—no regrets!).

JUNGLE JUDI

During the months we'd been on the Baja, my mom and Poncho (yellow lab) had settled into the jungle. Natural living clearly suited Jungle Judi. Her eyes glowed in delight as she skipped around, relieved to have us home and eager to get started with building the lodge.

"Work is great exercise!" she chimed. My mom has always radiated health, positive energy, and gratitude. The first eighteen years of her life in Alaska had made her tough and made her crave tropical living. She'd met my father in Anchorage, and when he'd introduced her to Mexico, she'd been smitten, by both the man and the place. The beaches, tacos, tequila, mariachis, and romantic Latin vibes were irresistible. Mexico quickly became her home away from home.

When my mom got her first glimpse of the jungle outside of San Pancho in 2004, it captured her heart. From there, the going was a bit rough. She says that the purchase of the property was "the most stressful experience of my life." My parents scraped together every penny of their savings and mortgaged their home in Quebec to buy the land. The financial challenge was exacerbated by the process of purchasing land as Americans in Mexico—long, frustrating, and perplexing.

JUNGLE JUDI—
TAILWIND JUNGLE LODGE

Hostess, yoga teacher, and community outreach
*"I have a deep fear . . . that at any moment I might
wake up from this dream that is my reality; a life in
this special place that is the Tailwind Jungle Lodge."*

What keeps you motivated and inspired?
From the beginning, I promised the universe I would do all I
could to keep the land natural; I committed to being a steward
of this incredible piece of jungle. I am continually inspired by
the birds and jungle creatures here. I'm also inspired by the
people who stay with us—their gratitude and excitement are
truly fulfilling.

Is the lodge today what you expected it would become?
In the early years, we worried about how we would get people
to come (and pay) to stay in this unique setting. The lodge has
exceeded my expectations! We now have clients lined up to
experience our unique place. This is truly my dream come true.

**What advice would you give to someone considering going into
business with family?**
I have learned that anything is possible. To keep an open mind
(composting toilets!). To go with the flow. To have faith in the
process.

**What do you wish you had known at the beginning of the cre-
ation of the Tailwind Jungle Lodge?**
Hindsight is always 20/20. Take your time. Building in stages
and learning the land helped us greatly.

✳   ✳   ✳

DIRTY FINGERNAILS

I traded in my salty Baja paddling attire for old work clothes. My wardrobe had certainly evolved since the uniform of kilts, knee socks, blazers, and ties I wore through high school. Garbed in the jungle version of dressing for success, I faced the daunting question: Where to begin our project? Where will *you* begin your project?

Our first priority was to familiarize ourselves with the land. Thus, the logical place seemed to be to build trails throughout the property—no easy task in the jungle. We promptly hired Jose, a local *machetero* (machete master) to help us. When Jose spotted me wildly hacking away at a bramble of vines, he gently removed the machete from my determined grip. Blistered and bleeding, I reluctantly let him take it. As I wiped sweat, grime, and twigs from my forehead, I watched Jose take down an entire bramble with one clean swipe. I determined that he would run the machete henceforth.

Don't be afraid to get dirty; go ahead and swing that machete a few times. Get a real taste of it. One of the joys of a small business is that you get to be involved in every aspect, test it out and see what you really enjoy. Don't worry, you'll get to point your finger eventually, but for now, revel in getting your hands dirty and learning along the way.

With Jose at work on the trails, my parents and I moved on to hauling rocks, a plentiful local material that we would use to build our stairs, trails, and erosion walls. Though our muscles ached with fatigue, the process of searching for stones allowed us to familiarize ourselves with the land. One thing was clear—our property is *very* steep. Gravity was a powerful force we could use in our favor. If you drop a coconut at the top, it will roll swiftly to the beach, down 300 vertical feet through five acres of dense jungle. You'll discover how to use the power of Mother Nature (biomimicry) in your business design in chapter 5.

Other questions popped up as we explored: *Which way did the wind blow? Where were the best vista points? Where were the most magnificent trees? How did the light come through the palm fronds?*

Where were the best places to build? As you begin to build and create, now is the time to explore and acquaint yourself with the foundation and building blocks of your wild business (whether it's physical or virtual).

The jungle gradually unveiled its wild personality. The shade of the majestic palms and a breeze off the ocean kept us cool. We were intrigued by the wildlife and delighted by the absence of bugs. It seemed to be a "friendly" jungle, but I could see there was much going on beneath the surface that was invisible to human eyes.

As I hauled bucket after bucket of rocks up and down Mother Nature's stairmaster, my legs strengthened and my determination did as well. Though the layers of grime on my skin thickened, my heart danced happily. My wild business was finally taking shape! How will you feel when your wild business is underway?

LOCATION, LOCATION, LOCATION ♥

Where you to decide to build, locate, and create will be the foundation of your wild business. Consider the following:

- Will my business need a virtual and/or physical location?
- If physical, what kind of space? Will I rent or own? Will I design my own space?
- Will I build it myself, retrofit an older space, or use something already established?
- What is my ideal location? Or do I prefer a movable office (van, Airstream, etc.)?
- Have I spent enough time in the proposed location, familiarizing myself with it?
- Will I do building work myself, or hire a local builder? Can I ask friends to help or trade services?
- Can I incorporate local materials?

- Can I afford quality materials or equipment? (This will save grief down the road.) Or can I buy used? Reuse is a great way to save dollars and the planet. (We bought used Girl Scout tents to use as our bungalows, and ten years later they're still working great.)

✳   ✳   ✳

A PLAN EMERGES

At the end of each day, I retreated to my tent, perched on the rooftop of my parents' casita. This tiny, flimsy-walled space would double as my home and office for nearly four years. You may need to make some sacrifices to get your business going.

Bits of paper and sticky notes—scrawled lists of ideas and to-do lists—were scattered between my sleeping bag and work clothes. My poor organizational system began to spill over into our daily work regime. Though my parents and I ultimately shared a vision of the jungle lodge we wanted to create, we each had different priorities, perspectives, and methods of getting there. Tasks were disjointed and unclear. Each day began with an exasperating three-way tug-of-war. Working by the seat of our pants would only take us so far. We needed a more concrete action plan.

FIRST BUSINESS MEETING

I called our first business meeting on November 1, 2007. We gathered on the rooftop by my tent/office. The original business plan I'd written in college had been usurped by our Baja business model, which focused on smart simplicity and mindfully slow and steady growth. We would build the lodge as a family, with no investors. With this new strategy, we needed a new plan. Wildpreneur Annie Kerr, founder of Wild Balance Jewelry says: "I can't stress the importance of having a plan; a researched, written down plan. Once the ball starts rolling, it's easier to tweak a plan than it is to find the time or mental strength to crunch the research and the numbers and lay the foundation as you go." You'll find some guidance on how to get started with a simple business plan in chapter 4.

In our plan, we assessed our projects, the pace of our progress, and set ourselves a deadline for completion—this date would also mark the official opening of the lodge. Make yourself a timeline and be specific with tasks to be accomplished. Fine-tune your project list, set short-term goals, and delegate tasks. As a family, we identified what we could do together and what was best to do independently. I wrote down our plan in pencil with an eraser on standby.

We muddled through the confusion and found order. At that meeting, El Tigre pronounced me "the Tailwind CEO." My parents had officially put me at the helm.

DREW CAPPABIANCA,
THE HUB

**Bike shop, café, and live music bar
in the New York Adirondacks.**

Is this work your passion? What keeps you motivated?
Yes. My work is really just an extension of me. The concept is mine, the execution is mine, the mistakes are mine. As a bike shop, café, and bar with live music, I often joke that I just turned my lifestyle into a job.

There's no limit to what we can do with the business. We can always do more (or less) and everything we do can always be better or different. We host charity rides and other events. We've added live music. We built a mountain bike and hiking trail system. We're starting a hostel. We've continuously refined our internal processes to make for a better customer (and employee) experience. What's next?

What's your favorite part about being a Wildpreneur?
Ultimately, at the end of the day, I'm in a situation that I got myself into by doing things I wanted to do. Good or bad. No matter how stressful it gets, I'm the only one responsible for putting myself in whatever position I'm in, and that's a freeing feeling.

Describe your perfect day as a Wildpreneur.
A perfect day for me is when one of our event ideas comes to fruition and succeeds. For example, we hosted a culinary bike tour of restaurants in the area a few years ago. A ton of time planning, promoting, and coordinating went into it. We had an unbelievable turnout, and everyone had an amazing time. There were a lot of moving parts and points of potential failure, yet it all came together. I'd like to stress the "everyone had an amazing time" part. There's no greater feeling than people expressing sincere gratitude for something you've created.

What was your inspiration to create The Hub?
I wanted to actually sell fun, regardless if you ride bikes. Everyday life is busy and hectic and stressful. I wanted to create a release from that.

Did you make any personal sacrifices to get your businesses started?
Do you mean other than constantly being on the verge of a mental breakdown, straining my marriage to the point of needing counseling, and nearly suffering an existential crisis? Seriously, all that happened, but on a lighter note I went from driving a 2013 Volkswagen Jetta SportWagen TDI to a 1990 Ford F150 without air-conditioning, heat, or a working radio, and that shook like a banshee above 45 mph.

BACKUP PLAN

My parents were enthused and ready to invest their time, effort, and finances into getting the lodge up and running. El Tigre had been a successful and experienced entrepreneur over the years. Though he'd put me in charge, there was one condition: This would be a trial period. Everything that we built had to be of practical use as a family vacation home should the business not go as planned. Though my parents believed in me, they insisted on having a backup plan. What is your backup plan?

ROUTINE

We settled into our jungle routine. Cool mornings were best for physical work, then I would dive into my online to-do list. With no Wi-Fi in the jungle at the time, this meant that I had to journey into San Pancho. I *dreaded* this twofold—screen time seemed unnatural in my jungle life, *and* I was terribly shy.

Regardless, I committed myself to at least one hour of internet time each day. I knew no one in town, and whistles and catcalls from the Mexican men made my cheeks burn a brilliant crimson as I searched for a quiet place to hide and work. A foolish quest indeed! Mexico is the land of noise—campo music, roosters, dogs, and trucks with blaring loudspeakers. I had no choice but to dive in and tackle my fear. Remember—you, too, may have to endure some situations that are out of your comfort zone: Go boldly forward, embrace the challenge.

I wedged myself into tight corners of cramped coffee shops and poached Wi-Fi from any house with an open signal. Though I struggled through my online to-do list, the town began to work its charms on me. San Pancho (its official name is San Francisco) is a classic coastal Mexican village with a laidback vibe. Its population of roughly three thousand fluctuates with seasonal expats. Cobblestone streets are shaded by banana, almond, and palm trees. The tantalizing smells of *pollo asado* (grilled chicken) and freshly made tortillas waft through town, laced with the intoxicating fragrance of tropical blossoms. Taco carts, coconut stands, and colorful souvenir shops decorate the streets.

Though I was unaware of it in 2007, San Pancho was on the brink of discovery by tourists and developers. My family and I were part of an early wave of expats. We'd had impeccable timing, positioning ourselves perfectly to accommodate the upcoming influx of visitors. There are certain market forces you can't control, but being at the right place at the right time is certainly beneficial for your business. Though we had fallen in love with the jungle, the rising popularity of the town of San Pancho has been a tremendous asset to our business. Was it fate? Have you noticed any synchronicities in your journey thus far?

POWER HOUR

I began calling my computer sessions "the power hour." With months of practice, I became a master of efficiency. I'd summon my laser focus and get my online work done in a flash. I almost unintentionally designed my business so that I could ultimately spend less time surfing the net, and more time surfing the waves. It's quality of work time that matters, not quantity. Build efficiency into your work ethic from the outset.

However, as the locals began to recognize me—my long blonde hair and light skin didn't go unnoticed in this town of Latin features—my power hours served another purpose. Curious minds, both Mexican and expat, would gesture at my computer and ask what I was up to. I blushed shyly as I clumsily stumbled my way through my elevator speech in choppy, awkward Spanish. To my surprise, locals were supportive and intrigued by my project. My voice grew steadier with each delivery. With practice, your confidence will grow.

WANTED: JUNGLE ADVENTURERS

Once I'd designed my own basic website, I was ready to broadcast the Tailwind Jungle Lodge to the world. In late October 2007, I hit the send button—releasing my first email newsletter to friends and family, announcing our opening day as December 15.

WANTED
ADVENTUROUS OUTDOOR ENTHUSIASTS!

LOOKING FOR ACTIVE PEOPLE WITH ADVENTUROUS VALUES WHO ARE INTERESTED IN ADVENTURING INTO THE MEXICAN WILDS

We are excited to begin hosting our first guests this fall and for our first season in business we're looking for pilot groups to help us refine our services and iron out the kinks. Come help us work toward creating the jungle and ocean experience of everyone's dreams! We're looking for groups (2–6 people, groups of friends, family, etc.) to make the trip to the Mexican jungle, stay for ridiculously cheap and help us refine our accommodations, tours, and services and promote us when you return home.

Please contact me, Tamara, for more information and let me know when you might like to come. Prices are negotiable and we guarantee an amazing experience!

❋   ❋   ❋

Hah! Not too bad. After all, I was only twenty-three with no marketing experience. Reading this now makes me giggle and cringe. Given my repeated use of the words *adventure, adventurer,* and *adventurous*, I was clearly captivated by the adventure of it all. This spirit was what kept me going. Good thing I was too young and inexperienced at the time to know better, I dove headfirst into the school of wild business where I learned on my own dime.

Within a few days, I received a response from a friend with whom I'd studied abroad in Australia. Her family had eagerly volunteered to be our first guests. We would have just enough beds to accommodate them.

READY FOR LAUNCH? ♥

Consider the following as you prepare to open the doors of your wild business:

- How will I attract my first clients or customers?
- How might I do a test run with my product or service?
- Would friends or family be willing to act as my guinea pigs?
- If I send out an email or newsletter announcing my business, who will I send it to and what will it say?
- Who are my targets—my ideal customers? How will I reach them?

＊　＊　＊

BUILDING NUTS AND BOLTS

With our guests due to arrive on December 27, it was time to get cracking! We devised a crazy pulley system to carefully lower beams and planks of chiche—a hardwood from the Mexican mountains—down two hundred stairs. Jose informed us that it is one of the densest types of wood imaginable, which also makes it highly resistant to rot and ridiculously heavy. Our tropical education was underway. Tune into local knowledge to discover which materials are best suited to your project.

With our two wooden decks on stilts complete, we erected a pair of 14x16-foot canvas tents that I'd purchased used from a Girl Scout camp. As these safari tents found their new home in the jungle, we designed and built composting toilets, then headed into town to scour the local markets for rustic style furniture and finishings. With that, our glamping-style bungalows were ready for action!

LA JEFA

Progress was underway on the upper part of the property as well. The Palapa Tigre (named after guess who?) would be slightly more up-scale and easily accessed. El Tigre designed the plans, then passed them over to a local builder, Adalberto Garcia. Though my father is a talented carpenter, this type of concrete and tile construction was beyond his capabilities.

Adalberto's dark Mexican features peered at us skeptically from under his cowboy hat. My father's natural building designs were foreign to him. Adalberto spoke no English, and my parents' Spanish was limited. This left me to decipher Adalberto's thick local lingo—far from the formal classroom Spanish I'd learned. Hand waving and blueprints filled in the blanks of our conversation. Yet it seemed that whether Adalberto understood me or not, he would nod his head "*si*," and do things how he thought best (Adalberto certainly accelerated my education in the Mexican way). Though Adalberto initially seemed perplexed to see a woman (me) managing a project in the jungle, he eventually nicknamed me "*la jefa*" (lady boss). My parents and I marveled at Adalberto's crew in action—no complex machinery, just manpower and creativity with only two speeds: on and off. They were either working hard or taking a siesta.

STONES

"*Mas piedras, chiquitas*! (more little rocks)," declared Adalberto. Hundreds of small stones were needed for the tile floors, counters/bars, and shower walls of the Palapa Tigre. There was just one problem—we'd exhausted our supply of rocks onsite.

"Let's go search the beach," El Tigre suggested. I readily agreed—my toes hadn't touched the sand in weeks.

As my parents and I loaded our buckets with beautifully colored stones, we frolicked in the tide pools, tossed the coconut for our dog, Poncho, to fetch, and laughed at the jungle debacles we'd encountered thus far. Take time to play with those who work alongside you.

NICK POLINKO,
RUMPL

Motto: Blankets for everywhere.
Light, compact, travel ready.

Your perfect day?
A perfect day to me is a balance between getting to do the things you LOVE (ski, surf, bike etc.) and willingly enjoy the things you NEED to do (work, grow, earn, learn etc.).

What do you wish you'd known?
The key lesson: you are the authority of your business. I think we are all used to being in a work environment where there is always a superior with the right answer, or just an answer to follow. This isn't true when you become a Wildpreneur. You have to learn to trust your gut and learn from the mistakes you will definitely make because no one (should) know your business better than yourself.

What was your inspiration to create Rumpl?
First and foremost, we created a product that WE wanted to solve a problem we had. We were outdoor guys who wanted to spend more time outside, not be cold, and not have to deal with dragging around a bunch of dirt and grass stuck to our blanket. The Rumpl Blanket solved that problem and we loved what Rumpl could mean for other people—enjoying more time outside in close proximity with the people you love. We had a product we loved that got people outside more often, so it was natural for us to be able to market and sell the blankets genuinely.

❋   ❋   ❋

PILOT GUESTS

On December 27, 2007, I paced the airport nervously. Our first guests were due any moment. The bungalows and the Palapa Tigre were ready—pillows fluffed just in time. After smiles, hugs and introductions, I loaded up their suitcases, and we were off to the jungle. I held my breath until we pulled up to the lodge and I escorted them in. When they grinned with delight, I was overcome with relief. The Tailwind Jungle Lodge was officially underway.

ALL-INCLUSIVE MISERY

"How am I going to make it through five more days of this?" I groaned as I collapsed into my tent, exhausted. Two days of hospitality had kicked my ass—hauling rocks had been a breeze in comparison. For these first guests, we had created an all-inclusive vacation package—we acted as cooks, maids, tour guides, bartenders, and more. This was no 9–5 job, this was 24/7.

We gritted our teeth and committed to making it through the week. Then things got worse. Midway through their stay, our guests got sick with the "tourista tummy bug" from some unfriendly street food. The sound of vomiting into our composting toilets echoed around the jungle. A teenager yelling "I HATE the jungle" echoed through the trees.

At the end of their stay, I handed them the proposed bill for the week. They looked at me and laughed. Saying that the price would be negotiable in my "wanted" ad had been a mistake. Expenses for food alone were significant, even before we considered our endless hours of work. The ride back to the airport was awkward and tense. Make pricing clear before you accept your first clients/customers.

CAROLYN BARNWELL, DOCUMENTARY FILMMAKER AND LIFE COACH

Motto: Let's get to the heart of your story.

What advice would you give to a potential Wildpreneur?
Starting is the hardest part. Think of everything as an experiment you can learn from, and take action. Then take another action and build momentum. It doesn't have to all be perfectly planned and strategized for you to start creating.

Do you have a mantra for your journey?
"The best way to predict the future is to create it." —Abraham Lincoln

What keeps you motivated?
I am fueled by joy and gratitude for being able to help people get to the heart of their story. It fills my tank, so to speak. My tangible sense of possibility and freedom keeps me motivated.

✴   ✴   ✴

BELLY FLOP

In my mind, our first guests had been a disaster. Instead of a graceful launch, our jungle lodge had done a giant belly flop. I drove home from the airport demoralized—the storm of my mind seemed more intense than any of the El Norte windstorms we'd experienced on the Baja. I fled to the beach where I sobbed so violently that the hermit crabs gave me a wide berth.

My mom found me, and we sat in silence as my tears pooled in the sand. When I could cry no more, she pulled me up, brushed me off, and walked me home. The next morning it took all my willpower to crawl out of my tent and call another business meeting. You will encounter setbacks; KEEP GOING. Persistence is the only way forward. In the famous words of Thomas Edison: "I have not failed. I've just found 10,000 ways that won't work."

MEGAN MICHELSON, FREELANCE WRITER WHO CREATED THE TAHOE MILL COLLECTIVE

A shared workspace for adventurers and Wildpreneurs.

What do you wish you'd known prior to creating the Tahoe Mill Collective?
That, sometimes, it'll feel like you're failing. Customers will go away, people won't pay their rent, and you'll get a huge bill for some electrical or plumbing problem and it'll feel like the whole thing is going to collapse. But then, something will happen: New customers will show up in droves or a newspaper will run a story on you or something. And it'll all turn around. And those up-and-down swings are just part of business. Don't fret over the little stuff.

✳   ✳   ✳

REFINING

Clearly, we were not cut out to be an all-inclusive resort. Some essential adjustments and refinements in our services would be necessary to make the business work for us. None of us loved to cook, nor did we want to play chauffeur (we now have much respect for chefs and chauffeurs). The solution? We immediately added kitchenettes to our bungalows (guests can make tacos in the jungle whenever they want), began to recommend local restaurants, and found a chef to cook for groups. For transport, we contacted a local taxi service and rental car company who were happy to offer their services.

My family and I now laugh at the pandemonium of that first week. We are grateful to that first set of brave guests—they taught us many lessons, primarily around pricing and the reality that we couldn't do it all. Being a jack-of-all-trades, master-of-none, is exhausting and inefficient. Though it had been useful for us to experience all aspects of the business, it was not sustainable. Pick the hats you want to wear. Once you've opened for business, assess the following as you go along:

- What am I good at? Which hats do I want to wear?
- How can I refine my services to suit my skills and interests?
- What part of my business wears me out? Where can I conserve my energy?
- What am I not so good at? Which hats can I delegate?

CAYLA MARVIL, LAMPLIGHTER BREWING

Craft beers made and poured at this unique taproom with café-like coffee setup.

What do you wish you'd known prior to getting started?
It's OK to find people who are better at things than you, and it's OK to trust them to take control of aspects of the business. In fact, it's more than OK—it's necessary.

What's your favorite part about being a Wildpreneur?
Making my own schedule and being my own boss. Being ultimately responsible for everything that happens is always both a positive and negative, but I wouldn't want it any other way. It's exhilarating, rewarding, and empowering.

Your perfect day?

There are lots of perfect days! Having a day where all opera-tions go smoothly is perhaps the most perfect (and the most rare). And any day that involves trying new beers that have gone brilliantly, or designing a new concept that we're all really excited about. And any day where amazing customers or friends or family come into the taproom, and I'm able to share our product and stories with them. And any day involving eating burritos, because burritos are the best.

✳   ✳   ✳

ARTFUL MISTAKE MAKING

The lessons continued (and always will!). Poorly tied hammocks sent guests crashing down, leaky tents, soaked beds, fridges attacked by *tejones* (local monkey-raccoon-type creatures), and so it went—a con-tinual comedy of trial and error.

"You know, failing is considered a badge of honor in the entrepre-neurial world," a fellow Wildpreneur reassured me.

"Well, if that's true, then I've got a trophy coming my way!" I said, laughing sarcastically, but it actually felt good to see the humor in struggle and prompted me to consider the silver lining of failure. Per-haps the torrent of mishaps would ultimately be a good thing for my business. I was enduring the school of hard knocks, growing stronger each day. Instead of feeling discouraged, I felt alive—empowered and eager to apply what I was learning.

No one should ever be afraid of failing; it's being afraid to give it your all in trying that I urge against. If there's one thing I've learned, particularly in my life as an athlete, it is that our limits may not be where we think they are. And, even when you think

*we've finally reached them, the next time we go exploring we
often find that they've moved again.*

—CHRISSIE WELLINGTON,
IRONMAN WORLD CHAMPION[6]

If mistake making is an art, then my parents and I are the masters.
The creation of the jungle lodge has been a perpetual game of one-
step-forward-and-two-steps-back. We've gotten things wrong more
often than right. When my parents and I attended my brother Rhett's
graduation from the University of Vermont in the spring of 2009,
the keynote speaker, Julia Alvarez, offered the following wisdom:

Mayan weavers have a prayer they say before they start their
weavings, done without a manual or set of instructions. The prayer
says, Grant me the intelligence and the patience to find the true
pattern. The work of doing and undoing is part of the work of
finding the pattern.

This wisdom was an instant favorite with El Tigre. I've heard him
repeat it countless times to guests over the years.

ANNIE KERR, WILD BALANCE JEWELRY, BRECKENRIDGE, COLORADO

**Designed for women with wild hearts.
Motto: Be entirely, wildly you.**

What do you wish you'd known prior to getting started?
There will be failures, but you just have to keep riding it out. It's
important to keep in mind that so much can change in a year,
a week, a day, a moment. This, too, shall pass, high or low.

What was your inspiration to create Wild Balance Jewelry?
The inspiration to start Wild Balance came from both my need to support my addiction to turquoise and also to scratch the itch of starting a business of my own, a reality that I knew was only a matter of time.

Describe your perfect day.
That's what makes this ride so wild is that no two days are the same. It's a beautiful thing! I wake up most mornings with a general outline of what needs to happen that day, but it typically morphs into its own reality, and I just have to roll with it. If the day involves sweat (preferably outdoors), good food, and some level of accomplishment, I'd say it's close to perfect.

Is this work your passion?
I've pretty much known that I wasn't going to be a 9–5er. I'm a manager's nightmare, full of opinions, questions, and "my ways." I consider myself wired to work for myself, which can be a blessing and a curse. My passion for finding a business to dedicate myself to, finding a need to fulfill and a purpose, has been my motivation throughout the roller coaster known as your twenties.

What keeps you motivated?
I'm fortunate enough to see what I create in action every day, which warms my heart and fuels my spirit. Women of all ages around my community sport Wild Balance earrings all over. Seeing my jewelry on the cashier at the grocery store or on a girl on what I know has to be a Bumble coffee date, or an earring spotted on a lady in the lift line, these are the moments that motivate me. I make jewelry for these authentic, everyday moments and pride myself on making these women feel good, beautiful, and somehow more themselves so they can carry on thinking about more important and fun things than their jewelry.

REWIRING
"FAILURE"

Why is it that failure often comes with a negative connotation, often perceived as shameful? There is no failure in the natural world, animals don't grapple with self-consciousness, there is only persistence, adaptation, patience, and innovation. Why are we humans so worried about failure?

Let's rewire our thinking around failure as artful mistake making: a positive force, a portal to success. Astro Teller—expert in intelligence technology—agrees. He advises us to run at all the hardest parts of the problem first, to chase after failure instead of fearing it. He explains that "Discovering a major flaw in a project doesn't always mean that it ends the project. Sometimes it actually gets us onto a more productive path."

Wildly successful entrepreneur Sophia Amoruso, author of the best-selling book #*GirlBoss* and founder of Nasty Gal, an online vintage-clothing boutique that rebounded from bankruptcy, says failure is our own invention. She challenges us to "dive headfirst into things without being too attached to the results. When your goal is to gain experience, perspective and knowledge, failure is no longer a possibility." From the inception of her business she has viewed it as a work in progress. "I constantly tweak and move on, peeling back layers of the onion as new ones arrive."

Source: Astro Teller, Ted Radio Hour, "Failure"

❋　　❋　　❋

GRIT

I've often wondered, what was it that propelled me out of the tent the morning after my first meltdown? Why didn't I quit?

Wildpreneurs are equipped with a little somethin' special: GRIT. Author Angela Duckworth explains that "what we accomplish may depend more on our passion and our perseverance than on our innate talent." Duckworth's words often echo in my mind: "I won't just have a job, I'll have a calling. I'll challenge myself every day. When I get knocked down, I'll get back up. I may not be the smartest person in the room, but I will strive to be the grittiest."

As you consider your own pursuit of Wildpreneurship, you may wonder—where does grit come from? Is it something you're born with? Something you learn? Some element of grit is likely a combination of both nature and nurture, but in the end, it's all in your head. You can make a conscious decision to get gritty. In the words of Henry Ford, "Whether you think you can, or you think you can't— you're right." You don't need an MBA to start your dream business, but you do need grit. Grittiness will allow you to rise to the misadventures that inevitably come.

So, here's the big question you must ask yourself now: Am I ready to call upon my grittiness? Summon your grit by saying a big YES to the following: ♥

- Can I stay focused?
- Am I a hard worker?
- Do I have perseverance?
- Can I be strong when challenged and work my way through obstacles?
- Do I finish what I begin?
- Do I have the support I need to stay committed to my project (friends, family, fellow Wildpreneurs?)
- Do my priorities and my wild pursuit align?

SHANNON HUGHES, PANCHO VIDA T-SHIRT SHOP AND TERRA MAR REALTY

*"Be stronger than your strongest excuse,
and when the going gets tough, never give up."*

What is the biggest obstacle you've encountered?
Myself. Learning to master fear and doubt is critical.

What is the best piece of advice you'd give?
Learn how to manifest. Have a vision, see your goals, and then learn how to make them happen.

What have you learned from living/working in Mexico?
Life can be beautifully simple. Most of us here don't have TV. Instead, we watch sunsets.

✳   ✳   ✳

NO PAINS, NO GAINS

You will not get everything right the first time around, you *will* make mistakes, and you *will* be uncomfortable. Embrace it. Above all else, summon all your grit—get up when you get knocked down, test, learn, experiment, focus. May artful mistake making propel you to success! Don't waste time feeling guilty or frustrated—"If you could kick the person in the pants responsible for most of your trouble, you wouldn't sit for a month," advised Theo Roosevelt. Instead of beating yourself up, look forward toward growth. With time, you will gain strength, expand your comfort zone, and "one by one these subtle refinements add up to dazzling mastery," reassures Duckworth. Now go get dirty.

EMILY AND COREY, WHERE'S MY OFFICE NOW—DIGITAL NOMADS AND LEADERS OF THE VANLIFE MOVEMENT

Motto: No return address.

"I love making it up as we go. It's always an adventure. And I LOVE being outside. It's home."

Thoughts on your journey?

We often receive messages like "I am so jealous" and "You are so lucky" and "I live vicariously through you." I just want to say that we are by no means "special." We didn't come from riches. We got a little bit lucky in the timing of the vanlife movement, but mostly we work really, really hard. For the first four years of vanlife, we didn't make a penny as influencers. We didn't even know what influencer marketing was—we were just living our dream and sharing our story. In the beginning, I worked as a web developer, Corey guided mountain biking tours, and together we worked on a farm. As Wildpreneurs, we must be willing to take risks, be uncomfortable, and be adaptable. It's always changing.

Describe your perfect day.

My eyelids rise with the sun, a whole new day. No alarm clock is needed. The swell arrived overnight, beautiful head-high waves that journeyed across the sea. I grab my camera and pretty much fly out of my 1987 VW van in awe of the sunrise. My lover, Corey, is right behind me, surfboard in hand. I skip around like I am ten, pausing briefly to capture the beauty I see. Pink lit puffy clouds. Miles of deserted sand beach. My dogs, running free. Corey catching a wave. I make breakfast in our tiny van kitchen and take a photo of the turmeric fried eggs. And then I surf. I surf and surf and surf. And when I can no longer paddle, I get out to write. Tomorrow we will drive one hour back to the closest town for Wi-Fi, where I'll check emails and post on Instagram. But today, today is a glorious day, and I am inspired to create.

Did you make any personal sacrifices to get your businesses started?
We sold vehicles and gave away our belongings. We traded the comfort of hot showers, a heated house, and a traditional 9–5 for the unknown of the open road. Experience over stuff is our aim. And it hasn't been easy. We've been completely broke, waiting for a paycheck to arrive. We dumpster dove for a period of time.

Advice?
Believe in your story. Know your strengths and your weaknesses. Make a plan and stick to it. Show up for yourself day after day. Keep your vibration high. Do what you need to do to be healthy and happy. There's a lot of work necessary to make your dreams come alive. Stay the course.

What do you wish you'd known prior to getting started?
I wish I knew the importance of alone time for my creative life. I wish I took more weekends for myself. I learned it's important to check in regularly and be honest about my needs. Often our rate of travel has been too fast for me and has led to stress and burnout.

What was your inspiration to create Where's My Office Now?
On a surf trip to Nicaragua seven years ago, Corey and I were inspired by the simple, adventurous lifestyle. We realized we hadn't experienced America and decided to live in a van as an experiment. Could we merge a nomadic adventurous life with a traditional 9–5? Really, we just wanted to surf and mountain bike and see America and thought we'd try to make it happen. In the beginning, we left the end date to be determined . . .

maybe we'd be on the road for six months. Or a year. Now we are six years in . . .

Do you have a favorite motivational quote or book?
One quote from *Women Who Run with the Wolves* by Dr. Clarissa Pinkola Estes that I love is, "The only trust required is to know that when there is one ending there will be another beginning," which seems to complement Nike's "Just do it."

✳   ✳   ✳

CHAPTER THREE

FINANCIAL ROLLER COASTER

WILD·PRE·NEUR
NOUN: WILDPRENEUR; PLURAL NOUN: WILDPRENEURS

WILD: LIVING IN A NATURAL STATE, UNTAMED

ENTREPRENEUR: A PERSON WHO ORGANIZES AND OPERATES A BUSINESS OR BUSINESSES, TAKING ON GREATER THAN NORMAL FINANCIAL RISKS IN ORDER TO DO SO.

WILDPRENEUR TRAIL MAP #3

Though money may not be the essence of what truly drives Wildpreneurs, it's a key ingredient. My journey of pesos and pennies has been a roller coaster of risk and strategy; a useful case study for Wildpreneurs. In this chapter, we will explore:

- The art of creative funding and living on a shoestring.
- Budgeting and reinvesting.
- Two job synergy.
- What is "enough" financially and personally.
- Smart lifestyle simplification.

As you get started, you'll likely encounter one large speed bump: money. Perhaps you have already asked yourself, "Do I keep my job and squeeze in work on my personal project on the side? Or do I dive in head first and focus all my energy on my wild pursuit?" There are many different ways to fund your dream—savings, day job, investors, partners, and even crowd funding. Wildpreneurs agree; there is no wrong way, as long as you're moving forward.

SHARED RISK

From the outset, my parents and I were partners in the creation of the Tailwind Jungle Lodge. We invested every dollar we could scrape together, shared the risk, and went for the "dive in head first approach." My parents took a mortgage on their home, and I put in the little bit that I'd saved from summer jobs. Though it was a pittance, it was terrifying to put my hard-earned savings into buying the canvas safari tents and funding our marketing efforts. Financial risk is relative—if you only have a thousand dollars and you invest the entire amount into your business, it will feel like you are taking big risk. Your risk will vary depending on circumstances such as partners, dependents, and so on.

Putting my own money and family money into the project fueled my determination to create a successful business. Investing money that you worked hard to earn is a highly effective commitment booster.

FINANCIAL LESSONS

I assumed responsibility for all of our finances. As guests began flowing through the lodge, I recorded all incomes and expenses and weighed the pros and cons of every costly decision. Some expenses were necessary and obvious—when my laptop fell out of the Jeep Wrangler and smashed onto the cobblestones, I ruefully paid to have it repaired, then ordered a bomb-proof case for it. Lesson learned, problem solved. Other financial decisions were more ambiguous. Do we pay a premium for higher quality building materials now? Or do we stick to our budget and compromise the longevity of our structures? How do we handle guest cancellations? Do we give credit or offer refunds?

Managing our finances was like trying to run a marathon while balancing an egg on my head. I took every step with extreme caution while also trying to move steadily forward. Though I pinched every penny, my parents' startup funds were quickly depleted. Within the first year, we were completely dependent on the income from the lodge to keep us afloat. One financial misstep would be a fatal blow to our young business. If I dropped the egg now, we would never get to the finish line without investors. As I policed our expenditures, I repeated to my parents, "We can't afford that. Maybe next year." Patience is key.

SHELBY STANGER, WILD IDEAS WORTH LIVING

Adventure podcast series and blog.

What do you wish you'd known prior to getting started?
I always wish I had and still am working on having more patience. Everything good just takes time, sometimes longer than you might want it to take. Also, that I'm never going to clear my inbox or get totally to the end of where I want to go. I just learned that recently, and the journey has been so much more enjoyable ever since I made this mind shift. I don't have to have things figured out. I don't have to have the right answers. I don't have to be perfect. Now I can have fun.

Did you make any personal sacrifices to get your businesses started?
I lived in Costa Rica when I was super broke, and it happened to be a good time to live in Costa Rica so I was pretty happy to

eat a diet of mostly rice and beans when I was younger. As long as I had good waves out front and plenty of coconut water, I was happy. Today, I don't eat out at restaurants too much, not just because it's expensive but I can cook better or healthier food at home. I don't go to many shows or buy a lot of clothes. I've found the best things that I enjoy are free—waves, running, love, and spending time with my friends and their kids.

The biggest sacrifice has been time. I am uber focused, so I'm not always available to hang out in the middle of the day, and I don't get many weekends off. I've just learned to say "No" to most things unless it's a "hell yes"—no to any B.S., no to negativity, and yes to only things that are meaningful and/or bring joy.

Advice?

Have a plan. Get a mentor. Write it down. And don't take everything so seriously. You are going to have to make decisions fast, so just do your best. Be nice to everyone. You never know who will be your next mentor or customer, even if you are surfing, so don't steal other people's waves (this is always a work in progress for me).

Also, be really kind to yourself. It's easy to become a perfectionist and to be overly self-critical when your business is your baby. If you can be really nice to yourself and have a sense of humor about the ups and downs, you will be able to fix things quicker and have more fun with your business, and probably be more successful, too.

What was your inspiration to create your podcast?

I wanted people to feel less stuck and to pursue their own wild ideas. The times I have felt stuck—when I was nervous to quit my job to pursue adventure journalism fulltime, the time I was scared to move to Costa Rica to teach surf lessons, or the time I moved to New Zealand with the love of my life—listening to stories of others who have taken the road less traveled and made positive decisions helped me feel a little less stuck and gave me the courage to pursue my own dreams.

Your favorite part?

I love that I have to be able to do multiple things so I am always learning, and that since I am the boss I have to own and take full responsibility for anything that goes wrong. That can be difficult at first, but taking responsibility frees up a lot of emotional energy that you might use blaming someone else. Unless you have an imaginary boss, you get to own it all. I also love that, for the most part, I get to work on what I want, when I want, with whom I want, that I miss traffic most days, make my own hours, and often work in my bikini or yoga pants. I've never owned a pant suit or blazer in my life.

✳   ✳   ✳

SEASONAL BUSINESS

We closed the lodge at the end of our first season in May 2008. We would be a seasonal business, closed in the summer time—torrential rains transformed our friendly jungle into Jurassic Park (think giant bugs, stinging plants, severe storms, mud, heat and humidity to extremes). We've become grateful for this annual routine. As the summer rains rejuvenate the lush jungle, we also take a break to rest, rejuvenate, and enjoy the freedom to explore other wild places. Integrate regular breaks into your business model: write "recharge time" in your planner as you would any other business commitment. Wild business may be 24/7 but you can and should take time off when you need—one of the beauties of working for yourself.

REINVESTING

At the end of our trial year, we assessed our finances. While we earned little income, we learned much about hospitality in a wild environment and a new culture. Our limited season meant reduced profit and the cost of maintenance and repairs in the jungle was above our expectations. These numbers determined that we had no choice but to reinvest all income back into the property—we made zero personal profit that first year. But at least it wasn't a loss!

As I proceed with my financial story, note once again that every wild business is different. Even two people setting up the same business in the same location may have a different financial approach and outcome. Personality, experience, circumstance, connections, creativity, and synchronicity will make each Wildpreneur's journey unique. There is no specific recipe; open your mind to the possibilities. Find the books, podcasts, stories, and people that resonate with you.

RHETT JACOBI, ARBOR CONSTRUCTION (TINY HOMES AND RENOVATIONS)

"Being 'captain' of the ship is a big responsibility, but the benefit is that you can steer wherever you want it to go . . . being self-employed is a gift that should never be taken for granted."

Have you made any personal sacrifices to get your business started?

Starting a business was the most challenging thing I've done. I'd say it took two to three years before those growing pains started to subside. My story . . . with a borrowed truck, and a rented trailer, I finally ran out of money (temporarily bankrupt) after dumping a load of concrete at the dump, with the trailer left there as collateral for what I owed for the dumping fee. I had to ask my employee's wife (whom I had never met) to loan me

$200 so I could finish the day's work. It was humbling. We laugh about it now and I still refer to her as my favorite "loan shark."

What was your inspiration to create Arbor Construction?
I saw starting a business that allowed me to take on "projects" as a way to maintain my freedom and not get stuck in the daily grind. I love being outside, using my hands, and interacting with people, so I thought that being a contractor would be a slam dunk.

How long did you think about starting your business before you actually did it? What was the tipping point?
It was a slow progression of learning how to build and getting the experience necessary to take the tests to become a contractor. Once I had passed the tests and actually had my contractor's license in hand, it was the same sensation as standing at the top of a ski run, or the high dive . . . now it was time to "drop in" . . . hesitating wasn't really an option.

✳   ✳   ✳

GETTING CREATIVE

With the lodge closed for the summer, I had four months of freedom to do as I pleased. My empty piggy bank made my philosophy of minimalist living (inspired by the Baja) a practical necessity. I needed a break from the jungle, but where to go and how to fund my life?

One serendipitous day, shortly before our jungle season came to an end, I was guiding some of my guests on a kayaking tour, and they mentioned they were from Boulder. Ding! The Rockies had captured my heart a few years back. By the end of the paddle, they'd offered me a job as a solar-panel installer in Boulder. Ding ding! From there, I found a housesitting gig, booked my plane tickets with air miles and headed to the mountains in early June. Synchronicity?

That summer, I lived off less than a thousand dollars. No car? No problem. I commuted to work by road bike. I feasted at happy hours (two for one appetizers!) with friends and when my house-sitting opportunities expired, I slept on couches. John Mackey, founder of Whole Foods reflects that "despite working many eighty-plus-hour weeks, Renee and I initially took salaries of only about $200 a month and lived in the office above the store. There was no shower or bath-tub there, so we took 'showers' in the store's Hobart dishwasher when we needed to clean up."[7]

I also got creative with my marketing for the Tailwind Jungle Lodge. Colorado is a hot spot for adventurers—my ideal target market. A love of mountains and ocean often go hand in hand—skiers are often surf-ers and vice versa. I passed out business cards everywhere, and I care-fully placed brochures at yoga studios and coffee shops around town. I did an unpaid internship with Sustainable Travel International, a Boulder-based nonprofit. This synergy turned into an effective market-ing outlet as they promoted the Tailwind Jungle Lodge on their website. Can you get creative with your marketing to keep startup costs low? Can you position yourself in a place where your audience hangs out?

My inexpensive lifestyle had even allowed me to save a bit that summer. I squirreled away this tiny sum to keep as an emergency cash stash. As soon as possible, put aside a small cushion, emergencies happen. What is your backup (oh shit) plan?

Be smart, think ahead, but don't let limited funds deter you. Wild-preneur Ford North explains that he was ready to launch his online company—a *Star Wars*–based mixed martial arts computer program for kids—but had a dilemma. He needed a steady source of income to pay rent, but working his day job wasn't leaving him enough time to get his business going. Solution? He and his wife quit their jobs, packed their bags and embarked on a year of WWOOFing (Willing Workers On Organic Farms) in Oregon. In exchange for their help on the farm for a few hours each day, they were given food, housing, and plenty of free time to do as they pleased. Ford's business is now well underway! Remember that vegetables grow in dirt, and you can get whatever you need at thrift stores.

PETER HALL,
HALA SUP BOARDS

Design. Adventure. Better.
Motto: Innovators in stand up paddle boards.
"I wanted equipment that didn't exist, tried to design it,
and then came up with the idea for a business."

What is the best piece of advice you'd give to a potential Wild-preneur?

1. Never pay with equity when you can pay cash.
2. Set your customers up for success. Make it easy to understand what you do.
3. Make your product really high quality OR make it really cheap but good enough. Do not play in the middle.
4. Say yes and figure out how to make it work.

✱   ✱   ✱

GAINING POSITIVE MOMENTUM

As we began our second season in the jungle, the wind at our backs was strengthening. Money was coming in more steadily, and we even boosted our rates. Guests were loving the lodge.

A neighbor, Isabella Scandolari, approached me on the beach one day. As her white garments fluttered gracefully in the ocean breeze, she explained that she was a Kundalini yoga instructor and asked, "Would you be open to hosting a yoga retreat at your place?" These words would alter the course of my business and my life.

TRUSTING THE FLOW

A year later, we hosted our first yoga retreat. Yoga By The Sea, led by Isabella, was a tremendous success, and I caught a glimpse of a new audience/niche for the lodge. Yoga retreats were growing in popularity internationally and a movement toward healing and purposeful vacations—opportunities to "disconnect to reconnect"—was on the rise. The Tailwind Jungle Lodge checked all the boxes for retreats seeking a natural destination. Hosting groups also made a lot of logistical sense; one big group would be much easier for me to manage. Keep your mind open as your business progresses and evolves, as new audiences and niches may present themselves. As my yoga retreats have taught me, let go of attachment to the end result. Though it's important to have a vision from the start, let things unfold and flow naturally.

WHERE THERE'S A WILL, THERE'S A WAY

"All the breaks you need in life wait within your imagination."
—Napoleon Hill

Creativity is a useful tool when it comes to funding—particularly in the early stages. There is an art to living on a shoestring. Some ideas for you:

High rent? Brainstorm ways to avoid this expense. Ask around for house-sitting opportunities, roommates, or move to a more affordable part of town. If you can work remotely, try WWOOFing, living on a boat, or in a van.

Own your own house? Consider renting it out. Try listing your place as an online rental. Holiday weekend or big event in town? Rent your house to vacationers and go camping! A short-term rental may be enough to cover your mortgage plus some.

Barter. Short on cash? Ask friends and local shops if they're willing to trade. I often trade stays at the lodge for farmers-market goodies, clothing from local shops, and more. Who might be willing to trade for the product or service that you're offering?

Recycle, reuse. Check out thrift stores before you buy new. You'd be amazed at the great stuff you'll find.

Brown bag it. Making your own food at home, or packing up meals to go is a great way to save $. Buy in bulk.

Find the best happy hours. Happy hours often offer BOGO (buy one, get one free) appetizers as well as drinks. Going out doesn't have to be expensive if you know where to go.

❋   ❋   ❋

REFLECTIONS: LIFE ON A SHOESTRING

Our whole business requires ingenuity. We used an air conditioner to create an improvised walk-in refrigerator. We gather rainwater to make ice to freeze and pack fish. We rebuilt a historic wooden fishing dory. You don't really make a living, it is a lifestyle. We do it 'cause we love it. We do it 'cause we need the river. —*Mike Wood, Su Salmon Co*

We launched our Kickstarter campaign with four working samples. As the campaign grew in popularity, news and media outlets kept calling asking if they could review our product for their publications (great!). However, we only had four samples and did not have the money from the campaign yet to place a real inventory order. Struggling between the option of getting huge press hits or having the few products in our hands to demo/photo/promote was a huge pain point for us. We would reluctantly send our blanket to the editors (who are used to getting tons of free samples) with a note: "PLEASEEE RETURN ASAP, This is our ONLY sample." When they didn't come back, we would cross off the products' names on a chart, fallen-soldier style.   —*Nick Polinko, Rumpl*

I created my first Life Is Beautiful calendar at Kinkos. I only had enough money to print fifty copies. But I love that it's grown organically, and the daily messages really resonate with people. As the business grows, there's more I want to create, but I've never gone the investor route. Just taking the next step (or leap) as it feels right. I've maxed out a few credit cards in the process of trying to make things from scratch, but it always seems to work out in the end.   —*Sarah Love,*
I Stand for Love Calendars

I actually started this business while I was on unemployment, with only a credit card and a recipe. I would go to all my friends' kitchens when they were at work, take all my ingredients and materials out of the car, and try to make all my bars before they came home. At one point, I remember my lunches were either peanut butter and jelly, or an avocado with some hot sauce on it. Even today there are sacrifices. Having a business is almost like being a parent. It takes all of your attention and energy, even when you are not at work.   —*Mike Rosenberg,*
Garuka Bars

Most times, my shoestring budget has led me to meeting amazing, generous people and unforgettable moments and places. It's taught me to be free and unattached. When you are living your dream, money isn't necessarily the priority. Your drive and passion take you to where you need to go, and you'll meet the people who will inspire you or give you a piece of advice that will help keep you going on the path toward your vision.   —*Natacha Radojevic, Moana Surfing Adventures*

BUDGET ASSESSMENT AND REINVESTING

The Yoga By The Sea retreat leaders were eager to bring more groups to the jungle. However, there was one prerequisite: More beds were needed. As we prepared to close for our second season, we studied the numbers and determined that the majority of our income would be reinvested into the property (and not our pockets, once again) in order to expand our capacity and build several more casitas. We were on the brink of financial viability—the ability to accommodate retreats would lead to profitable long-term possibilities for the lodge.

While our future vision was clear and bright, my immediate personal situation was not quite so rosy. After laying out an updated financial plan for the coming year, I ended up with a check for $1,000 USD. Break that down to an hourly wage, and we're talking pennies, but it was more personal profit then I'd earned the year before. Progress!

When I'd first arrived in the jungle, the colorful peso bills that came and went felt like monopoly money. Now, as I handed over thick stacks of those hard-earned bills to Adalberto (our master builder) and other service providers, this no longer felt like play. Building projects went over budget, and unplanned expenses popped up. Expect to go over budget. Plan for the unforeseen.

As your wild business begins to bring in money, you must find a balance of profit and reinvesting in your business. Though it may be tempting to pocket profit, reinvesting in your business is essential for growth and increased income down the road. The nature and scope of your business will determine how much you reinvest. Find your balance and proceed accordingly. Assess and adjust as necessary; there is no set rule here.

During the first five years of our wild business, my parents and I reinvested the majority of our income. Our slow and steady mentality (without investors) and significant building costs made this approach a necessity, while our minimalist, low-expense lifestyle made it a possibility. Now that we've reached our ideal capacity, we still invest approximately half of our profits into the Tailwind Jungle Lodge annually. This works for us in the jungle, but again, find your balance and what works for you.

CROWDFUNDING AND MICROFINANCE?

You don't need a "pile of cash" to get going. Starting small and growing steadily is a smart approach that is often more sustainable. The largest trees start out as tiny seeds!

Need that little bit of capital to get started? Consider the following:

1. **Crowdfunding:** Why not get support from friends, family, peers, and/or fellow wild businesses who believe in your idea? Find funding for your business through a variety of online crowdfunding platforms.
2. **Microloans:** Micro lenders specialize in loans under $50,000. Research SBDCs (Small Business Development Centers).

"When you're getting started with your wild business, I highly recommend that you read a lot, sleep a lot, and get a loan! Oh, yeah, and don't start your business on credit. Take it from me, credit truly is the devil your dad warns you about. Use that plan to get a lower interest loan and pay it off!"   —*Annie Kerr, founder of Wild Balance Jewelry*

✳   ✳   ✳

BLOSSOMING

Within a few years, we'd expanded our accommodations to sleep up to sixteen guests, an ideal capacity for diverse retreats—yoga, meditation, fitness, aerial silks, and more. Retreats from around the globe began steadily flowing through the lodge. As their inspirational energy floated through the palm trees, the lodge found its personality and blossomed. Our financial situation gained momentum. We continued to infuse money into refining our accommodations and services. Our priority: guest comfort and happiness. Our goal: for each guest to fall in love with the Tailwind Jungle Lodge (this is the key to word-of-mouth business).

JAVIER CHAVEZ, WILDMEX SURF & ADVENTURE SCHOOL

*"Don't let people tell you your dreams are not possible.
If you work hard enough, you'll make it happen."*

What is the best piece of advice you'd give to others looking to start their own unique business?
Make sure it brings money in before making a big investment. I have seen so many people come to Mexico and invest $50,000 in some business. Just four months later, they'll have their bags packed, ready to go because things did not work out. For example, if you want to sell T-shirts, rather than opening a nice, big shop on the main strip, start small. Find a shop that has some extra floor space where you can sell your products for a commission. With a setup like that, you can test to see if the product is popular and go from there.

What was your inspiration to create Wildmex?
Since I was a kid, I had always enjoyed traveling, nature, and sports in Mexico. On a trip through Australia, New Zealand, and Indonesia, I realized that there were places in the world where people were actually making a living out of their passions like surfing, camping, biking, and so on. That motivated me to do something similar in Mexico.

ENOUGH?

This approach was working! As the lodge and our guests thrived, I was delighted by our success. Yet, instead of celebrating this hard-earned accomplishment, I collapsed into the tent that had been my home for years. The demands of hospitality were taking their toll—I was exhausted and depleted. My inner truth knew that professional success had come at a cost beyond monetary. While our guests enjoyed jungle bliss and comfort, I lived out of a backpack and slept in a sleeping bag. As our business had flourished, my basic living situation had been neglected. Consequently, my health was deteriorating—I didn't have the time or the space to take care of me.

With this realization came denial and inner turmoil. *My business is my priority*, I reminded myself as Turbo Tam plowed onward. This is not the time to focus on me, I resolved: *This tent is all I need. Or is it?* As I gazed at the flimsy walls of my tent, my inner dialogue deliberated: What is "enough?" *Minimalist lifestyle is part of my identity, but perhaps I've taken it too far? Has my shoestring budget pushed me out of my comfort zone into unsustainable territory with personal and professional consequences?*

Couplepreneurs Paul Girardi and Danielle Hachey, founders of Feathers & Fur Retreats, have also weighed the pros and cons of ultra-simplistic living on a shoestring. They reflect on their transition from living as vagabonds chasing waves to putting down roots, buying a home, and starting their own business:

> Life is pretty easy when everything you own fits in a van, your only priority is timing the swell to its best daily potential, and no one expects anything from you—life as a free agent was pretty cruisy. There are times when it seems like passing on that vagabond life was a sacrifice, but truthfully, it's nice to be accountable and productive and actively creating a life rather than just floating through one.

PERSONAL LIMITS ♥

Gently pushing yourself out of your comfort zone financially may be necessary in order to fund your business. There are many ways to cut corners. Some sacrifice may be necessary, but ultimately, we're seeking a reasonably comfortable quality of life. If you venture too far out of your comfort zone and find yourself consistently living in the anxiety zone, this is an unsustainable and unhealthy place to be. Feeling chronically anxious is a signal that you need to slow down and reassess. Be mindful of your basic personal needs: Your long-term happiness and success as a Wildpreneur are at stake!

WHAT IS ENOUGH?

Take a moment to draw some attention to your personal limits:

- If I'm living on a shoestring in order to fund my business, how long do I plan to do so?
- What is a reasonable timeframe to sacrifice a healthy living situation?
- What are my basic needs?
- What do I really need to live comfortably? See chapter 7 for guidance around taking care of yourself.
- What is home for me?
- Do I need an additional source of income to meet my basic needs?

TOO MUCH?

Also consider the other end of the spectrum: "Do I have too much?" In our modern world, many traditional entrepreneurs are programmed to constantly seek more: We work more so we can make more money so we can buy more things. Is this really necessary? Though I needed to upgrade my living situation to find balance in my life, some may find balance by downsizing. More money and more stuff don't necessarily lead to happiness.

✳   ✳   ✳

PERSONAL BOUNDARIES

Gallery owner Cori Jacobs recalls that in order to get her business started in Sayulita, Mexico, she moved out of her apartment and into the studio where she worked. For months, she didn't have a kitchen and showered at friends' homes in order to trim extra expenses. Though this was a necessary measure in the beginning, she has since learned the importance of having a living space that is separate from the gallery—that division between her workplace and personal space is essential. She says: "Self-care is the best care. Investing in yourself is the best way for you to have the energy and enthusiasm to keep your business alive." Today, the Cori Jacobs Gallery is a colorful cacophony of paintings, pottery, and clothing. As her business thrives, Cori is happy in her casita several blocks from the gallery.

WALLY WALSH, CERVECERÍA ARTESANAL

Craft beer 100-percent Mexican made.
*"I love the lack of monotony and not working
to fulfill someone else's dream."*

Did you make personal sacrifices to get your business started?
When we sold our early-1900s bungalow in Portland, Oregon, and moved to Mexico, I didn't envision living in a 350-square-foot

studio apartment for the first twenty months, but we sacrificed in order to put resources into starting the cervecería . . . and it has paid off.

Advice?
1. Do your research.
2. Think of the worst possible things that can happen, and honestly ask yourself how you'd respond.
3. Listen to both kinds of people: those who think you can't fail, and those who think you can't succeed. It's good to hear reasoning from both sides.
4. Don't worry about trying to control things that are outside your immediate realm of influence.

What was your inspiration to create Cervecería Artesanal San Pancho?
Never having to drink a commercial Mexican beer ever again! Wanting to promote the up-and-coming generation of talented and passionate Mexican craft brewers. Offer San Pancho something unique, in terms of quality, aesthetic, and a vibe where craft beer lovers from all over the world come to congregate and enjoy sharing stories over a pint . . . or three!

Your favorite motivational quote or book?
"Movement is life. Life is a process. Improve the quality of the process and you improve the quality of life itself." —Moshe Feldenkrais

❉　　❉　　❉

HITTING PAUSE: SOLITUDE AND RECALIBRATING

As the yoga retreats flowed through the lodge and celebrated the jungle as a place to retreat for healing, wellness, and balance, I felt like a fraud. My inner voice berated me: *Who* am I to promote the Tailwind Jungle Lodge as a healing retreat center if I can't even take care of myself? As I repeatedly collapsed into my tent, I feared that everything we'd worked so hard for might collapse as well. It was time to pause, reassess, and consider the interplay between my financial choices and personal comfort. "The cost of a thing is the amount of what I will call life which is required to be exchanged for it, immediately or in the long run," said Henry David Thoreau.[8] In other words, the price of anything is the amount of life you pay for it.

At the end of our second season, my parents returned to Quebec for the summer, and I moved out of my tent and into the Palapa Tigre. I was in no state to go anywhere. Thus, I intentionally isolated myself in the jungle and decided it would be my personal retreat to find clarity. From my comfy new perch, I experienced my guests' perspective on the jungle and fell in love with the natural paradise all over again. My body and mind relaxed for the first time in months, and I opened my heart to the healing powers of the jungle.

I rejoiced in the quiet solitude and enjoyed weeks without social interaction, grateful for the unscheduled time. One evening, as the lightning of an intense summer storm flashed around me, clarity struck—life in a tent was no longer "enough." I had three urgent financial and personal needs in my life.

- Additional income. The financial pressure of those startup years had been a tremendous weight on my shoulders. Though I prided myself on my ability to "rough it," living on an extreme budget had taken its toll.
- Home. Using my tent as an office and a living space was no longer enough.
- Health. I needed my vital energy back. I craved nutritional knowledge and guidance.

PERSONAL AND FINANCIAL TRANSFORMATION

After nearly two months of jungle solitude, I ventured out to seek solutions. The Colorado Rockies beckoned once again, and I found myself in a friend's Telluride kitchen sipping green juice. As this liquid life force flooded my veins, I was introduced to the wonderful world of whole food living—dark leafy greens, colorful fruits and veggies, sprouted nuts, seeds, raw foods, and more. As I feasted from local farms that summer, I came back to life, and a solution to my dilemma emerged.

That fall, I enrolled as a student at the Institute for Integrative Nutrition. Through their distance learning program, I studied holistic health. Simultaneously, the program trained me as a health coach. Bingo. I'd found two solutions—I could continue to run the lodge and have a supplemental income as a health coach.

Thus began my year of personal and financial transformation. As yoga groups flowed through the jungle, I happily joined them in celebrating healthy living. I launched my Jungle Girl Health coaching practice and began working with clients via Skype. When a friend offered me her closet in San Pancho as an office for my calls, I eagerly accepted. Surrounded by musty storage containers, I was thrilled.

TWO JOB SYNERGY

For the next few years, I simultaneously managed and developed both the lodge and my health coaching. With only so many hours in a day, I had to create a synergy between the two businesses. I offered holistic nutrition workshops to my guests at the lodge, and promoted jungle retreats to my health clients. My businesses fueled each other, win-win!

Don't hesitate to juggle two jobs at once. Many entrepreneurs keep their "day" jobs while creating their dream jobs. According to Adam Grant, author of *Originals*,[9] studies show that "entrepreneurs who kept their day jobs had 33 percent lower odds of failure than those who quit." He also points out that covering our bases financially gives us the freedom to be original without pressure. Famous author Stephen King worked as a teacher, janitor, and gas station attendant for seven years after writing his first story, only quitting a year after his first novel was published. King was certainly a lesson in patience and perseverance.

The word "entrepreneur," as coined by economist Richard Cantillon, literally means "bearer of risk." However, this isn't always true. If you're risk averse and have some doubts about the feasibility of your wild business ideas, you may prefer to proceed mindfully, slowly, and steadily (while working your day job). By this approach, your business may ultimately be better built to last.

If you do decide to juggle two jobs, use concurrence in your favor. Consider ways that your day job might complement your entrepreneurial pursuit, even beyond financial support. Combine marketing efforts for your day job to gain experience that will support your Wildpreneur vision. If you are planning to start your own coffee shop, you may take a job as a barista in order to gain experience. Internships are another useful gateway to experience and networking.

However, if you're working two jobs, don't be half-assed. Your clients and customers will only take you seriously if you take your work seriously. Can't juggle two jobs at the same time? Take a sabbatical or figure out some way to ensure that you can give 100 percent.

DAN ABRAMS, FLYLOW

A skier who imagined better gear for the mountains.

Advice?

1. **Be mindful that every conversation could lead to something beneficial.** It could be a stepping-stone or a connection that could change the course of your business.

2. **Perseverance** is the greatest determination of success in business. Be patient. When you've never done this before, you have no idea how the story is going to unravel.
3. **Appreciate when things are going well.** Don't dwell on the bad stuff! Move on.
4. **Slow down, you don't have to do everything right now.** If you don't focus on the essential tasks at hand, you won't be able to do any of them.
5. **You don't need to be everything to everyone.** It doesn't work like that. Especially if you're bootstrapping it.

Any thoughts on getting started on a shoestring?
Hah! Bartending was part of my recipe for success. In 2010, I'd been bartending for eight years, and Flylow was six years old. My Flylow CFO finally told me that, in September, we would have enough to start paying me a salary. On August 27, I took my last shift at the bar. At the end of the night, I walked to the corner of the bar, took off my bar clothes and threw them in the garbage can. I was done.

* * *

SMART SIMPLIFICATION

In 2011, I thanked my loyal tent and packed it away. It had served me well for five years of jungle living, but it was high time to unpack my bags. As I decorated the walls of my tiny casita, I felt like I was *finally* home. Hard work pays off.

September 2013 brought my thirtieth birthday. This milestone triggered another momentous life pause. What did I see? I'd created two successful businesses. Though I was proud and grateful for both, my immediate response to "How are you?" was "I'm busy." I'd spent most of my twenties rushing around, focused on productivity—no daisy sniffing allowed. Work had monopolized my time. I was living the antithesis of my dream life.

The question "What is enough?" loomed again. Good financial news at our end-of-the-season business meeting for the lodge sparked another life decision. It had taken seven years, but Tailwind was *finally* making enough profit to support me comfortably. With this happy realization, I thanked my health practice, and let it go.

I dove into the following season feeling inspired, healthy, and eager to give my dream business my full attention once again. I also vowed to live by a new mantra: Work hard and play harder! More time surfing the waves, less time surfing the net, right?

CASEY DAY, POWDER FACTORY SKIS

The world's finest powder skis, precision crafted in Colorado.

Advice?
Get a job in a similar business to gain some experience first, then you can learn from others' success and mistakes.

Your favorite part?
Answering to nobody and having complete control. If you make a mistake, there is no one else to blame but yourself, and any success you achieve is extra rewarding. If you need some vacation time, there's nobody to ask. You have the freedom to choose your own path through life.

Any personal sacrifices to get your business started?
The first year that I spent building skis in Silverton, Colorado, I moved seven different times over the course of the year. I lived in everything from wood-heated miner's cabins to a doublewide trailer heated by coal to a ski-in-ski-out condo to a

17-foot retro camper parked in a secret location by the side of the river. Oh, and I definitely sacrificed some sleep! Taking on other jobs during the day and starting a business with the remaining time at night doesn't allow for much sleep.

Is this work your passion?
My passion for skiing began as a young kid growing up in Colorado and has given me a direction in life ever since. Powder Factory Skis allows me to create as an artist and designer, as well as spend my life in the mountains as a dedicated skier.

✻   ✻   ✻

CHAPTER FOUR

WILDPRENEURSHIP 101— NUTS & BOLTS

FOR THE SIMPLICITY ON THIS SIDE OF COMPLEXITY, I WOULDN'T GIVE YOU A FIG. BUT FOR THE SIMPLICITY ON THE OTHER SIDE OF COMPLEXITY, FOR THAT I WOULD GIVE YOU ANYTHING I HAVE. —OLIVER WENDELL HOLMES, SR.

WILDPRENEUR TRAIL MAP #4

Your journey as a Wildpreneur will be much like a long-distance expedition. Though our businesses may vary in shape, many core elements are the same. This chapter pulls together all the basics, the essential nuts and bolts you'll need in order to live by the scout motto, "Be prepared!" What you choose to incorporate is up to you.

❋   ❋   ❋

My journey as a Wildpreneur began in a class at Middlebury College called "Entrepreneurship 101." In Vermont's Green Mountains, I wrote up the business plan for a jungle lodge. Though the class gave my dream career some much needed shape and direction, it didn't adequately prepare me for the journey ahead. I felt as though I was using the wrong recipe—traditional business tools wouldn't suffice.

More than a decade later, I've created my own version of that class, specifically designed for you, my fellow, free-spirited Wildpreneur. Be warned: Wildpreneurship 101 is not your typical business class, thank goodness. We're far from typical thinkers.

Instead of getting geared up in a business suit with a briefcase in hand, your journey of Wildpreneurship is going to require considerably different equipment. You'll soon be embarking on an expedition, venturing into the wilds where uncertain terrain awaits. With this in mind, what are the essentials you'll want in your backpack? Choose one of the following:

- Cast-iron frying pan
- Machete
- Hardcover novel
- Bug spray
- Duct tape
- All of the above

Carefully consider the functionality, practicality, efficiency, necessity, and simplicity of each item. Every adventurer will have different priorities and needs for the journey. My top choice from the list above? Duct tape. Mexico—the land of the quick fix—has taught me its multipurpose wonders. Machete and bug spray are close behind in utility. Heavy frying pan and hardcover novel? Ditch 'em. There are much smarter, less cumbersome alternatives. You'll be cursing that extra weight a mile down the trail.

STEP 1. CHOOSE YOUR ADVENTURE

Remember the *Choose Your Own Adventure* kids' books,[10] where you got to assume the role of the protagonist and make choices that determined the outcome of the plot? This is your real-life opportunity to design your life adventure. As you stand at the bottom of this mountain of potential, this is no longer a fairy tale—decisions now will affect the direction of your life.

As we did at the beginning of the book, start by brainstorming ideas and possibilities to determine the terrain, vehicle, and schedule that suit you the best. "When it comes to idea generation, quantity is the most predictable path to quality," says Adam Grant in *Originals*. Eventually you will stumble on your home run, but first, spend time on the daydreaming stage.

Once you've chosen your adventure, pick a catchy name. We began as Tailwind Outdoor and evolved into the Tailwind Jungle Lodge. A name can say so much about a business. For us, shifting our name allowed for a much more appropriate description of who and what our business had become. What will you call your wild business? Choose wisely; you'll be saying it a lot.

STEP 2. FUN PRIORITY

Make fun a priority from the beginning. "Starting a business worth starting is inevitably going to be a long hike, so you better find a way to enjoy it," says Jordan Silbert, founder of Q Drinks.[11] "Make having a good time a high priority for you and your team. I've learned that one of the biggest risks you face as an entrepreneur is giving up because the struggle is not worth it—everything is going to be harder and will take longer than you expect when you're starting out. But if you're willing to push on long enough, you will usually win. So figure out a way to make it fun." Schedule fun into your calendar as you would any business commitment.[12] You can write in pencil (things always change!) but adding it to your schedule will bring you one step closer to making it a priority. As Jungle Judi says, "Sacredness in revelry." It's never too soon to celebrate—focus on the journey, not the destination.

STEPHANIE GAUVIN, CANADIAN LANDSCAPE PAINTER

Is this work your passion?
Yes. This is the way I communicate; it is definitely my passion. Painting, for me, is forever. In addition to painting, I channel my energy and love for being alive by singing, skiing, bike riding, dancing. . . . You'll find me walking on my hands, cartwheeling . . . and I want to learn to unicycle, too!

Where do you find inspiration for your art today?
Every day, I am out in nature. I notice so many details, I think as a painter, I see the colors in nature and wonder how I will mix them in my palette to get them right, I wonder how I will interpret the beauty that my eyes see onto the canvas.

✳   ✳   ✳

STEP 3. RESEARCH
Before you hit the trail, do your homework. In this modern world, we have endless resources at our fingertips. Explore other wild businesses with a similar theme to yours and google your idea. As you design your adventure, you don't have to reinvent the wheel. Use the wheels that already exist and add your own twist. It's absolutely OK to imitate before you innovate. What you are doing will ultimately be unique as you infuse your own style and personality into your business.

RESEARCH CATEGORIES

- **Fellow Wildpreneurs:** Have other adventurers done something similar? Leaders in your field are an excellent source of guidance and wisdom.
- **Industry:** Familiarize yourself with your field—research trends, major players, risks, and sales data.
- **Ideal Customer/Target Market (Your Tribe):** Research demographics, geographic location, profile, how needs are or are not being met.
- **Products and Services:** Research what you will be offering. How will it be developed, produced, created, offered, and/or distributed?
- **Operations and Management:** How will you structure and manage your business? How have others done so?
- **Feedback:** Engage your fellow Wildpreneurs; they may be your best evaluators. Given their own adventures, they are likely open to seeing the potential in unusual possibilities and will give you honest, useful, and objective feedback. Find your devil's advocate.
- **Social Media and Email:** Test the waters by sending out an email or posting your proposed adventure on the social media platform of your choice. Poll your existing network to gauge interest and guide your research.

Source: *How to Do Your Own Market Research*

✳   ✳   ✳

STEP 4. SUPPORT: FIND YOUR YODA

Every good adventurer needs support from the get go. While friends and family are crucial, tapping into the wisdom of a good coach or mentor is another key ingredient to success. When it comes to mentorship and coaching, there are many forms (casual, formal, paid, etc.). Be mindful of whom you choose. A paid mentor or coach will charge a price for these services (this typically makes the commitment more serious and professional for both the teacher and the student, whereas an unpaid mentor or coach will be more informal and relaxed). The type of support you need will depend on your personal needs—career transitions, strategic thinking, accelerating change, goal setting, accountability, and so on. Having an accountability buddy is another great support system.

"Find your Yoda," says brew master and successful entrepreneur Jim Koch in *Quench Your Own Thirst*. He recommends finding "the very best person in the world" to mentor you and help you achieve your best. Of course, the very best person in the world is up to you to decide. One of my personal mentors is an eco-lodge owner a few miles up the coast from me. When you're searching for a mentor or guide, seek out someone who can relate to your experience and has some history in your field. A good mentor will share his or her knowledge with you and be an excellent sounding board. Find someone you trust and with whom you feel comfortable.

Prior to getting started, I wish I would have known the importance of mentorship. During a yoga-teacher training, I was "assigned" a mentor who ended up being the absolute perfect fit for me. I learned (and am still learning) so much from this amazing woman, twenty-five years older than me, more than three decades of experience in my industry. What a gift that was, being paired with her.

—MANDY BURSTEIN,
ZENGIRLCHRONICLES

DEREK LOUDERMILK, THE ART OF ADVENTURE

Podcast host, business coach,
and author of *Superconductors*.
*"The journey of a Wildpreneur is never boring.
There will always be more to learn."*

How do you integrate your experience as a former pro cyclist in your business coaching?
You must be mindful of the long-term nature of entrepreneurship. In the endurance world, you won't be hitting your fastest times in running or cycling until you have seven years of training under your belt—there are physiological adaptations that happen slowly over time. Then there is the mental aspect—you need to go through dozens and even hundreds of hard workouts to really understand your own strength. Both of these things apply to life as a Wildpreneur—you need to slowly change your thinking by changing the physical structure of your brain to be more confident, resourceful, resilient, collaborative, and so on.

Get really comfortable doing things that you have never done before. There are so many diverse skills in entrepreneurship, you are guaranteed to feel uncomfortable sometimes. Have a beginner mindset and be in it for the long haul. When I was a pro cyclist, I knew that a good season didn't come down to one great day of training, or even a month. It's about maintaining a high level of energy and fitness over many months while continuing to improve and progress. Think of the productive output of the greats like Picasso, Leonardo da Vinci, the Beatles, or Mozart—they were producing a ton of high-quality output for decades.

Wildpreneurship as an endurance expedition . . .
When you climb a 10,000-foot volcano for ten hours, every-thing else seems easy. When you tackle your biggest chal-lenges, you know how much more you can do.

✳　　✳　　✳

STEP 5. SPECIALIZE AND SIMPLIFY

Choose one summit instead of an entire mountain range. Many peo-ple don't specialize because they're worried about limiting themselves. However, if you specialize—hone in on your tribe and niche—you give yourself a chance to go deep, get creative and become a master of your trade. For example, if you're creating a restaurant, start by defining the type of food you plan to serve (Thai, Indian, Tex-Mex, etc.), and then specialize by identifying a few excellent dishes. This will reinforce your reputation for quality and attract hungry custom-ers, whereas loading the menu with mediocre options may leave ta-bles empty. Start small and simple, then grow from there. Avoid "lazy simple," embrace "profoundly simple." No short cuts, just smart de-sign. Don't hesitate to hire on help if you need it! Your business will suffer if you spread yourself too thin.

With smart design in mind, build your business on quality when-ever possible. "It's worth it to spend a little extra (if you can afford it) to get something that's just right," says Sophia Amoruso, trend-setting Wildpreneur and author of *#GirlBoss*.

JEN HINTON, CARVE DESIGNS

Bikinis and surf attire for active women.
"Hire people who know more than you. You can't do it all.
Plus, you can learn so much from them."

What keeps you motivated?

I walk into the office and there's a new challenge in front of me that we need to figure out. The people we have involved in the business—everyone brings something new to the table and keeps it interesting.

What was your inspiration to create your wild business?

"It all began on a surf trip to San Pancho, Mexico. As we lounged in a hammock waiting for the waves to roll back in, we lamented how hard it was to find board shorts that could keep up with us—real women with real bodies and a real passion for adventure. And just like that, Carve Designs was born.

Anything else you'd like to share?

Enjoy the ride!

❋　　❋　　❋

STEP 6. MISSION STATEMENT

Craft a mission statement from your heart and soul. If you truly believe in what you're doing and your purpose, the journey ahead will flow much more naturally. A clear, concise mission statement will set your intention, open the doors of synchronicity, and define your purpose. Our simple mission statement: Create a place for adventurers to reconnect with themselves and delight in the natural world.

Once your mission statement is clear, repeat it aloud to bring it to life. Practice your "elevator speech"—a synopsis of your business idea that is short enough to recite between floors in an elevator (approximately 30 to 60 seconds). It doesn't have to be rigid or formal; find a comfortable style that works for you. Marketing starts now. Take advantage of interested ears. Share your dream with others! Who knows where it may lead?

NUTSHELL BUSINESS PLAN—WORKSHEET ♥

OVERVIEW

What will I sell?

Who will buy it?

Why is my product or service needed?

MONEY

What will I charge?

How will I get paid?

ROGUE MARKETING

How will my tribe discover my business?

How can I get my tribe to tell their friends?

GOAL

One year from now, my business will have _____ (number of clients? income?).

Five years from now, my business will have _____ (number of clients? income?).

CHALLENGES

I foresee challenges with _____,
but I believe the solution may be _____ (fill
in the blanks).

(Repeat this section for as many concerns as you may
have.)

Further resources: There are infinite books, websites,
apps, podcasts, newsletters, and magazines for entrepreneurs.

✻　　✻　　✻

STEP 7. MAP AND COMPASS

Just as a map and compass would keep you pointed in the right direction, a business plan will give you clarity, guidance, and direction.
What is your ultimate destination? This map will give you a tangible
plan to share with others (particularly important if you're planning
to work with partners) as well as a clear platform for discussion and
springboard for the work that lies ahead. Need some guidance? Try
the "Nutshell Business Plan" worksheet to get started.

If your business plan doesn't feel right the first time, don't rush it!
Procrastination may actually be beneficial here.[13] The tendency to
delay could help Wildpreneurs build businesses that last. If you have
the gift of time, try being a mindful tortoise instead of a speedy hare.

Remember that every good plan is accompanied by a backup plan
in case of emergency. Should all fail, it's good to protect yourself. You
might even create a bailout plan, too. For example, if for some reason,
you are unable to continue running your wild business, could someone step into your shoes, or would it be possible to sell the business?

STEP 8. ITINERARY

Design your itinerary by incorporating long- and short-term goals into your business plan. These goals will guide you toward your ultimate vision, as well as give you motivation and organization in the short term. Use a clarity chart♥[14] to break down goals into smaller steps. For example, if you want to open a yoga or fitness studio, look at the big picture first: location, number of students, shape of the space, and so on. Then break that large goal down into smaller action steps that are practical and achievable.

Every year, sit down and write out your five-year dreams. In the yoga world, we call this a bhavana, a Sanskrit word meaning "calling into existence." Different than journaling, this is a powerful, concentrated, spiritual cultivation practice that time travels you half a decade into the future. . . . Write a letter to yourself five years from now describing how the last decade of your life has unfolded. Don't be shy! Don't play small! Go big. This is a practice of being bold and asking for EXACTLY what you want. We must always keep articulating and manifesting our biggest goals and dreams in order for them to come true!

—MANDY BURSTEIN,
ZENGIRLCHRONICLES

Of course, goals only work if you stick with them. In addition to the support of a mentor, a life coach or business coach can make a real difference.

CLARITY CHART
BIG PICTURE/LONG-TERM GOALS

GOAL #1   GOAL #2   GOAL #3

ACTION | ACTION | ACTION | ACTION | ACTION | ACTION | ACTION | ACTION | ACTION
STEP | STEP | STEP | STEP | STEP | STEP | STEP | STEP | STEP

SHORT-TERM ACTION STEPS

SMART GOALS

SET LONG-TERM GOALS

Within the next six months, what do I want to achieve with my business?

In the next year, where do I want my business to be? The next five years? The next ten years?

Next, focus on the short-term steps that will bring you closer to your long-term goals. A useful approach to short-term goals is to use the SMART acronym: Make your goals **S**pecific, **M**easurable, **A**ttainable, **R**elevant and **T**ime bound (or Trackable).

SHORT-TERM GOALS

What steps can I take today to bring myself closer to my goal?

What steps can I take this week?

What steps can I take this month?

Go through the questions above again, this time to set financial goals, then again with short-term action steps.

Source: *Management Review*, 1981

✳   ✳   ✳

STEP 9. LOGO/WEBSITE

Feeling artsy? Come up with an image or graphic to represent you and your adventure. You'll want a logo that is eye-catching, distinct, and relevant to your business name. Our logo began as a palm tree, then we added a wave and a spiral. After many drafts and feedback, it evolved into a graceful fusion of the three—a clean design that is simple, easy to replicate (make it easy to paint yourself!), only two colors (blue and white), and loved by our guests! Take a look at some of your favorite logos. What draws you to them? Plaster your logo on all aspects of your business—your website, newsletter, business cards, stickers, and so on. Implement the exposure effect—the more often people encounter your logo, the more likely they are to remember it.

Your logo is the beginning of your brand, which is essentially what people think of (factual and emotional) when they hear your name. Design your brand to let your unique flare and charm genuinely shine through. "Had I tried to fit in, Nasty Gal would have crashed and burned a long time ago. The last thing the world needs is another boring person or another boring brand, so embrace all the things that make you different . . . don't you dare alter your inner freak," says Sophia Amoruso in *#GirlBoss*. She adds, "When you accept yourself, it's surprising how much other people accept you, too."

Put your logo at the top of an awesome website. Your website represents the core of your brand, the face of your business, so design it wisely. Are you going for classy, spunky, artsy, personal, cool, sexy, fun, family? Pick your theme and breathe your personality into it. Consider your favorite companies. What makes you like them? How have they designed their website? Work with a graphic designer to create your website, or do it yourself. There are many simple platforms for do-it-yourselfers.

WEBSITE TIPS

Organized and easy to navigate. People are generally drawn to simplicity. When you place two comparable products side by side with the same components, people will choose the easier one. The design of your website can create a competitive advantage.

Font. Choose a legible font that suits your style, but keep it simple. Avoid fonts that are illegible with too many fancy flourishes.

Pick a suitable color. "You can open almost any magazine and see several ads that use beautiful washes of blue to market everything from tropical or ski vacations to the latest offer from Best Buy or Bed Bath & Beyond," says Wallace J. Nichols in Blue Mind. Why? Nichols quotes neurosurgeon Amir Vokshoor: "Due to its specific wavelength, the color blue is known to trigger a calming, relaxing, yet energizing effect." People are naturally drawn to the color blue, a marketing advantage. What color works best for your brand?

Images. Properly placed and captivating photos are more descriptive than a thousand words.

Videos. Keep videos short and sweet. Nearly 50 percent of viewers move on after a minute.

Concise and clean. Don't bombard the viewer with too many words, information, or hectic graphics.

Mindful wording. The word "adventure" is key for my jungle brand. Know your business and be honest and clear about what you're offering. What are your key words?

Search engine optimization (SEO). Help Google find you. Repeat key words in your website but don't overdo it—six times is memorable, too many times causes burnout (like listening to a song on repeat). SEO is worth researching and doing well.

Use the power of design. Airbnb founder Joe Gedia modified the design of the company website to build trust between strangers. Notice that the Airbnb website projects the feeling of "homey," easy to use, friendly, and welcoming.

Source: https://learn.g2crowd.com/video-marketing-statistics

❋ ❋ ❋

STEP 10. BE A ROGUE MARKETING MASTER ♥

No money for marketing? Don't fret. Here are my top tips for rogue marketing:

A. Be Uniquely You. Being authentic, shameless, and genuinely believing in what you're doing comprise the cornerstone of effective marketing. You won't sound "salesy" if you're speaking your truth. Be yourself—let your charm and personality shine. Find the marketing style that is most comfortable for you, and you'll most likely stick with it. Consider the following:

- Direct contact: Are you most comfortable speaking directly in front of an audience, leading, or joining an event with face-to-face contact? This works best for extroverts.
- Indirect contact: More of an introvert? Try blogging, podcasts, photos, or magazine articles, newsletters, and so on.
- Social media: Which type of social media works best for you? Facebook? Instagram? Twitter? Pick one or two of these platforms and do it well. Though social media is an

important element of your marketing platform, don't make it the foundation—it's more of a booster. Social media can be fickle—it changes rapidly and is difficult to keep up with. Growing your newsletter list is a much more valuable long-term strategy. Studies across the board show that selling through social media dramatically underperforms selling through email lists.[15]

ASHLEY WILLIAMS, RIZZARR

Social media platform connecting millennials with inspiration: Share your thoughts and make an impact.
"I hope that RIZZARR can be a powerful force in inspiring young people to grasp the powerful ripple effects that they can create."

What is the best piece of advice you'd give to others looking to start their own business?
Trust your gut and believe in yourself. Never lose sight of that vision. Realize that you can make an impact. For each of us, anything is possible as long as you believe, you work hard, and you never, ever, ever give up! You will encounter rejection, naysayers, delayed plans, and more, but just commit to that "never give up" attitude. The bad times did not come to stay, they came to test you, strengthen you, and they will pass if you stay committed and determined. Never back down without fighting for your dream.

What do you wish you'd known prior to getting started?
I never knew how much patience, persistence, commitment, and, most of all, perseverance one would need to start a business. It takes soooo much of all these things. I also wish I would have realized that, when you look at the most successful people, it's not always that they were the smartest, but, most

likely, they were the most committed and driven to make their vision a reality.

✳   ✳   ✳

B. Know Your Target. Who are your ideal clients? Where do they hang out? How can you connect with them? What kind of information are they most receptive to? Marketing efforts are much more effective if you know your target audience and put yourself in their line of sight. Consumers look for brands they can relate to, who speak to who they are. The best way to do this? Be your target! Walk your talk. Use your product or service yourself. If you don't use your own product or service, why should they?

C. Be a Storyteller. Bring your tribe into your experience from the first step. Share your project, goals, even your imperfections. People love real life stories! This will entertain, engage, and invite your audience to join your adventure. Derek Loudermilk, author of *Superconductors*, explains that, "Telling powerful stories helps your audience see you as relatable, real and trust worthy, which is necessary before you sell them anything."[16] Furthermore, story-brand expert Donald Miller explains, "Businesses that invite their customers into a heroic story grow. Those who don't are forgotten."

D. Freebies. Everyone loves free swag. Print your logo on practical items—hats, reusable bags, water bottles, T-shirts, and so on. As your clients use these items daily, happy thoughts triggered might prompt them to tell their friends about their experience with your product/service. Giving a freebie away on your website (e-book, coupon code, buy-one-get-one free, etc.) is also a great way to grow your tribe.

E. Customer Loyalty. Treat your customers/clients like royalty. They are your golden marketing squad. If they have an awesome experience, they will return and spread the word. Personalized thank-you notes (when possible) and discount cards for future purchases are thoughtful ways to follow up with past clients. After a guest has stayed with us, they are part of our jungle family. We offer a generous family discount as well as free nights to referrers.

MEGAN TAYLOR MORRISON, DANCE ADVENTURES AND ENTREPRENEUR COACH

Dancer, traveler, podcast host, coach, and creationista.
Motto: Uplevel your passion business.
"Wildpreneurship requires massive surrender,
trust, and strength. It is a divine journey."

What advice would you give to others looking to start their own wild business?
Talk to your customers. Talk to your customers before you start. Talk to them after they've used your product/service for a little while. Talk to them after they've used your product/service for a long while. If you focus on making your customers blissfully delighted, your business will grow. Your referrals will be off the chain! Remember, you have a relationship with your customers. They want you to win. They want you to delight them. In addition, get two times the amount of support you think you need. There is never enough support when you are starting a business. Half of becoming successful is expanding your capacity to be with much more support. Get started now!

What do you wish you'd known prior to getting started?
The first few years you hustle. There's no way around that. You need to hustle to build the momentum to carry you. Just because things aren't working yet is 0 percent indication that you're failing. Keep moving, keep talking to your customers, and keep creating strategic partnerships that light you up.

✳   ✳   ✳

F. Get Sponsored, Synergize. Seek mutual exposure. Team up with food and gear companies that complement your adventure. In doing so, you'll both broaden your tribes, a win-win! I've synergized with Boga SUP boards, Athleta clothing, Garuka energy bars, Carve Designs, Mika Yoga wear, Greenplus nutritional products, and others. These collaborations have allowed us to grow our businesses together. I also synergize with a nearby eco-lodge—we send each other guests regularly. Who might you collaborate with?

G. Go Green and Become a Holistic Business. Don't green wash, be the real deal. Now more than ever, people support companies that align with their personal values. We made a serious commitment to green business in 2009 and became the first certified sustainable eco-lodge in Mexico.[17] How can you green your business, minimize your impact, and give back? (See chapter 5 for more ideas.)

MIKE ROSENBERG, GARUKA ENERGY BARS

Handmade energy bars in Vermont, using local raw honey and 100-percent recyclable packaging, and 1 percent of our profits go to mountain gorilla conservation. Motto: Healthy food makes you happy.

"It's cliché, but it's true, a person who loves what they do never works a day in their life."

Is this work your passion? What keeps you motivated?
We make energy bars, but really what drives me is connecting with people and helping them enjoy their adventures. Having a delicious and healthy snack can really top off a great hike or bike ride. I love knowing that the bars we make go on amazing adventures with people all over the world. It's like a little piece of us gets to go with them. People send us photos of themselves with their bars on volcanoes, in the rainforest, on the ocean. It's just awesome to see the places the bars make it to.

What was your inspiration to create Garuka Bars?

I had hurt my knee and was going stir crazy, so I turned my attention to the kitchen and to becoming a better cook. I learned to make a bunch of different things, but once I was healed up, I kept making the energy bars because they were so useful in my active backcountry lifestyle. Really though, it was my friends that finally convinced me to do something with the bars.

* * *

H. Wise Spending. If you're going to spend money on marketing, be smart, go for maximum returns. Consider Google Adwords[18] (geographically targeted, pay-per-click advertising), newsletters services such as Constant Contact or Mail Chimp (start free, then pay a fee once you exceed a certain number of subscribers, absolutely worth it), and print materials (quality color brochures make all the difference). Also try donating your product or service to fundraisers—you will incur hard costs, but gain exposure and support worthy causes. We've donated stays at the Tailwind Jungle Lodge to a variety of different festivals in Colorado (where our target market loves to hang out).

STEP 11. BUILD YOUR TRIBE, NETWORK, AND SYNERGIES

Tap into the power of personal connections, this will never go out of style. Family, friends, and everyone you meet on your journey may become part of your tribe. Whether you're hiking a mountain or sitting at a coffee shop, you never know who you'll encounter. "It's not what you know, it's who you know," goes the saying. Start building your network with personal connections now and this will set the stage for easy marketing later. Make up some business cards pronto and carry them with you ALWAYS. Whenever you give out a card, ask for contact information in return and follow up whenever possible to deepen the personal connection. From social media to chitchat on a chairlift at a ski hill, there are infinite ways to network. Find what comes most naturally to you.

MINDFULNESS PAUSE: CHEAT SHEET TO GET STARTED NOW ♥

Though we're covering a lot of ground, getting started is actually fairly simple.

Follow these six steps:

1. Decide on a product or service.
2. Identify your client or customer.
3. Set up a website or a way to get the word out.
4. Create a special promo offer to attract attention (freebie or discount).
5. Establish a way to get paid (PayPal, cash, credit card, etc.).
6. When you're ready, launch! Don't wait until everything is perfect—perfection doesn't exist.
7. Enjoy the ride and learn as you go.

Source: Chris Guillebeau, author of *$100 Startup*

✳   ✳   ✳

STEP 12. BARTER

Trading is one of my favorite perks of Wildpreneurship. We have traded stays at the lodge for work on our website, photos, promo videos, organic veggies, clothing from local galleries and more. These trades have led to new relationships and beautiful synergies between wild businesses. How, what, and with whom can you barter? Note: If you're a natural giver, beware, not everyone is as giving as you are—be cautious and make sure that trades feel fair and expectations are clear.

STEP 13. FAKE IT TILL YOU MAKE IT

You won't always know what you're doing—mistakes are guaranteed—but if you believe in yourself and go forward with confidence, you will endure and gain respect in the process. Dress and walk like a pro, and you will become one. The only way to really learn is by trying things out. "Don't underestimate how much behavior affects your thoughts. It's easier to act your way into a new way of thinking, than to think your way into a new way of acting. Become an expert by living it," says author A. J. Jacobs, who is best known for his lifestyle experiments.[19]

KATIE VISCO, ULTRARUNNER AND CHEF

Run Across America and Run Across Australia/Hot Love Soup and Good JuJu Energy Balls
"I aim to work smart, thus cultivating time to explore wonders outside of work."

Advice?

Put what you need and want out into the world. If you need an investor, put it out there. If you need some pro bono marketing help, put it out there. If you simply need a mentor to chat with every once in a while, put it out there. Ask for help! This asking has opened up so much for me, and humbled me as well. I/you cannot do it all. Through asking, I've learned to trust others, build relationships, and, most important, foster my own audacity to share my art—business ideas, writings, events, goals, foods I've made for sale, anything originated in the deepest part of you—no matter what.

What keeps you motivated?

My relationships. My joy for life. My curiosity. My deeply rooted desire to leave the planet better because of my (relatively tiny) influence. I believe that, with community, anything you dream of doing will be noticed . . . and can make a difference.

Your favorite motivational quote or book?
I have given away all my books . . . except my mother's 1950 copy of *Walden* by Henry David Thoreau. I was recently asked why it's the only book I've kept; it reminds me that "all I need is all I got," which is my favorite quote.

✻　　✻　　✻

STEP 14. JOURNAL/NOTEBOOK

A name, idea, book, connection, website—write it down. You think you'll remember, but chances are you won't. Bring a notebook with you everywhere (your cell phone's notepad works, too, if you're techy). Your notes and records will also help you see patterns in your business down the road.

STEP 15. $ PSYCHOLOGY

Once you've created a quality service or product, put a price tag on it. Give it the mirror test: Look at your reflection and quote your price. If you can't gaze confidently into your own eyes, then the price needs to be adjusted. Price too low and your clients won't value your service enough (people find more value when they pay for something). Price too high and you'll turn people away. Play with your prices. Take a look at what similar businesses are charging to get a sense of the marketplace. Be sure to consider your expenses. Go from there and adjust as necessary.

Focus on money abundance, not scarcity. Be generous with others (within reason), and it will come back to you. I tip all of my employees and service providers regularly—my water and propane deliverers, maids, landscapers, and others. Giving them a few extra pesos and taking a few moments for a friendly chat makes them feel valued and inspires them to give me quality service. Bonus: The best way to save? Reduce your expenses. It's not all about making more. It's about being smart with your financial decisions.

MONEY TALK ♥

How will you determine the price of your product or service?

What will you charge friends and family?

Will you have a sliding scale?

What are your basic expenses?

Can you manage your own budget, or do you need help?

What are your short-term and long-term financial goals?

Tip: Use your business plan to pull these financial pieces together.

✽   ✽   ✽

STEP 16. FEEDBACK AND TESTIMONIALS

As your adventure unfolds, tune into the thoughts, wants, and needs of your clients/customers. Don't be afraid of criticism. Instead, perceive it as a gift—a way to enhance your business. Not all feedback will be useful, but you'll lose nothing by asking. Collect testimonials, too. Testimonials from happy clients are of paramount importance to creating trust with future and potential clients.

STEP 17. PLAY BY THE RULES

Though we're wild, we also want to be legit. Figuring out how to create a business in Mexico—the land of endless photocopies and office mazes—has been the ultimate test of patience. There may be less red tape, but there sure is plenty of frustration! Hiring someone to help me wade through the legal requirements (and translate) has saved me tremendous grief. Wherever you establish your wild business, figure out what you need to make it official. Pay taxes, get permits, collect receipts, and keep good records. It's not all fun, but it has to be done. Entire books and essays have been written on business ethics and the law of rules.[20] Start out correctly and you'll be grateful down the road.

STEP 18. OUT OF THE OFFICE (PERMANENTLY)

Build freedom into your business. If your cell phone is always on, your clients will forever expect immediate service. Instead, why not design a business that offers a timely response and quality product or service while also maintaining your quality of life? During my early years in the jungle, quick response wasn't physically possible—I had neither internet nor cell signal. Consequently, I implemented a permanent auto-response assuring email inquiries that they would receive a reply within twenty-four hours. My relationship with my guests/clients became one of trust and quality, not high-speed living. Set your phone aside often, turn your email off, live outside of the hyperconnected, speedy, sleep-deprived world. Arianna Huffington writes: "Our relationship with email has become increasingly one-sided. We try to empty our in-boxes, bailing like people in a leaky life boat, but more and more of it keeps pouring in. How we deal with our email has become a big part of our techno-stress."[21]

STEP 19. WORK SMARTER NOT HARDER

Work smarter not harder—build this mantra into your business model from the outset. Being busy doesn't necessarily equal success.

"Life doesn't have to be so damn hard . . . most people, have spent too much time convincing themselves that life has to be hard, a resignation to a 9-to-5 drudgery in exchange for (sometimes) relaxing weekends and the occasional keep-it-short-or-get-fired vacation," says Tim Ferriss, author of *The 4-Hour Workweek*.[22] Greg McKeown, author of *Essentialism*,[23] reiterates that there is a "point at which doing less (but thinking more) will actually produce better outcomes." Thus, it's not the quantity of time you put into your work, it's the quality of the work time. Work to be your best, not your busiest. "I used to have a 9-5 (or more like 8-6) desk job in a corporate culture where sitting at your desk proved to your boss that you were working (even if you weren't)" recalls freelance writer Megan Michelson. "So now that I work for myself, my whole goal is to be as efficient and productive as possible so I can be at my computer for as little time as I can."

Use the following techniques to work smarter:

Prioritize. Focus on a few essential to-dos and ignore the rest. "Being selective—doing less—is the path of the productive. It's easy to get caught in the flood of minutiae," says Ferriss. Lack of time is actually lack of priorities.

Deadlines. Create and respect deadlines. Are you a procrastinator? Or perhaps a precrastinator (tasks are done well ahead of time)? Is it better to be a tortoise or a hare, like Leonardo da Vinci who toiled fifteen years on the *Mona Lisa*. Experiment with both, but take caution with extremes.

Power hours. Are you a morning person or a night person? When is your mind clearest and most productive? Find the time of day when you do your best work.

Get organized. Workspace, computer, to-do lists, keeping things neat and tidy will support your work flow. You won't have to spend the first half hour of your day figuring out where everything is. Find an organizational system that works for you, your desk, your devices, and beyond.

Focus. Instead of working distractedly for three hours, concentrate for one hour on one task, then take a break. Avoid what technology writer Linda Stone, who coined the term "email apnea," calls "continual partial attention."[24] Minimize multitasking and turn off the constant information flow (news, social media, weather, surf reports, text messages, alerts on your phone, etc.).

Nap. Never underestimate the power of a siesta. Nap rooms are even being created in the offices of Google! Not a napper? Reset and clear brain fog with breathing, mindfulness, yoga, or meditation—the ultimate everyday performance enhancers.[25]

Movement. "Methinks that the moment my legs begin to move, my thoughts begin to flow," said Henry David Thoreau. Try the philosophy of *solvitur ambulando*: It is solved by walking.

Pick your sombrero. Once you've tried on the many hats of your business, pick the ones that you're best at. Get good at pointing your finger as you hire on help, contract outside provider services, and so on. Don't try to do it all. You're not always the best person for the job.

PROCRASTINATORS BEWARE

Giving yourself more time to complete a task gives ideas time to marinate. Consider the Sue Garnic effect—the usefulness of leaving a task incomplete. Garnic says: "We have a better memory for incomplete then complete tasks. Incomplete tasks have to stay active so we remember how to pick up where we left off. Your brain continues to work on it." This can be good for the process and the end result.

✳   ✳   ✳

A GRACEFUL SUM OF PARTS

With these essential tips and tricks, you'll be well prepared for the adventure ahead. Think of your wild business as a sum of smaller parts that work gracefully together. Repeatedly return to the simple tools in this chapter. Stick with it (persistence!), and you will find your path. As my brother, Rhett, says, "Un-sheath your samurai sword, stand for what you believe in, and be ready to work for it." Bring on the adventure and see ya on the trail!

When we persistently align ourselves with our deepest callings and desires, we can attract what is needed to do what we really want to do. When we live from heart-space, there is always a way.
—CAPTAIN LIZ CLARK[26]

CHAPTER FIVE

MOTHER NATURE'S WISDOM & BIOMIMICRY

WE CAN SEE, NOW MORE CLEARLY THAN EVER BEFORE, HOW NATURE WORKS HER MIRACLES . . . DOING IT NATURE'S WAY HAS THE POTENTIAL TO CHANGE THE WAY WE GROW FOOD, MAKE MATERIALS, HARNESS ENERGY, HEAL OURSELVES, STORE INFORMATION, AND CONDUCT BUSINESS. —JANINE BENYUS[27]

WILDPRENEUR TRAIL MAP #5

In this chapter, we venture into the essence of the wilds. Prepare to:

- Befriend a snake and work with nature instead of against it.
- Journey to a secret garden where we'll meet a biomimic.
- Discover how designs and strategies by nature offer tremendous guidance to Wildpreneurs.
- Explore a new philosophy: holistic business.♥

I thought it was love at first sight, but it wasn't. Lust at first sight? Absolutely. The land cast its spell over me instantly with its gracefully swaying palm trees and flirtatious blossoms. But the reality of actually living in the jungle? Far less sexy. When the time came to spend my first night in the tropical wilderness, my anxiety skyrocketed. *What creepy crawlies were out there? What might be lurking in the dark?* I was tormented by nightmares and restlessness until dawn. This uneasiness came as a surprise to me. I'd spent most of my life outside; a true tomboy. But for a girl from Quebec, the Mexican jungle was new territory.

A LOSING BATTLE

I awoke one night to find mysterious dark squiggles on the white walls and ceiling of my casita. I rubbed my eyes. *Am I dreaming?* Alarmed, I grabbed my glasses and hit the light switch. Ants—an exodus of thousands moving in highways throughout my casita. *Invasion!* I grabbed the garden hose and declared war.

I drenched every inch of my jungle home that night, but I was no match for this natural force. The ants displayed unwavering resilience. Despite the torrent of water, they recovered and rerouted their course within minutes. After a few long hours of war, I collapsed into my bed, exhausted and defeated, my only consolation being that at least the ants hadn't acquired a taste for bamboo sheets. The next morning, I was shocked to find that though the puddles remained, not an ant was in sight.

I continued to battle the wildlife—crabs, cockroaches, June bugs, dragonflies, and more. I also became well acquainted with the *tejones*—monkey-raccoon-type animals. Apparently, *tejones* love human food. These clever and dexterous nocturnal creatures quickly discovered our open-air kitchenettes—the goodies of my unsuspecting guests at the lodge were easy prey. *Tejones* relentlessly rattled fridges, rifled through cupboards and even managed to unscrew the lids off of peanut butter jars.

Attack! Once again, I prepared for battle. I passed out slingshots and encouraged my guests to defend their kitchen territory with stones. *Welcome to the Tailwind Jungle Lodge, here's your weapon!* Guests looked at me bewildered. Clearly, this wasn't an acceptable solution.

As I deliberated over the situation, a greater realization hit—my series of squabbles with wildlife allowed me to see that with my fighter's approach, I may win some battles, but I would always lose the war. The laws of the jungle ultimately prevail. I also began to observe that all these creatures have similar cycles. They arrive in alarmingly massive throngs but pass through quickly. Though I tried my best, I repeatedly learned that fighting their rhythms is of no use. With this in mind, I finally asked myself, *why not work with the natural flow, instead of against it?*

ALEXANDRO PERAZA AND FLOR FELIX, NECTAR HEALTH

Retreat chefs at the Tailwind Jungle Lodge.

What do you wish you'd known?
Alex: You cannot leave any food out in the kitchen of the Palapa Tigre overnight. My first time cooking in the jungle, the *tejones* (monkey-raccoon creature) ate all my superfoods!

Your favorite part about life as Wildpreneurs?
Flor: Working in the jungle is one of the most wonderful experiences of my life. I feel connected to nature. It feels like home. I love being part of the jungle family! Working at the lodge keeps me inspired and drives me to always give the best of me. I also love meeting the retreat guests. Many have turned into lifelong friends.

What was your inspiration to create Nectar Health?
Flor: After ten years working as a nutritionist in the city, we

were ready for a new lifestyle on the beach. We opened a healthy food restaurant in San Pancho, which sparked our taste for cooking and conscious eating. That evolved into the creation of Nectar Healthy Foods, a catering service company with vegan and vegetarian dishes. The name Nectar was inspired by purity, natural essence, and elixir of life (Nectar = drink of the gods, according to Greek mythology).

Anything else you'd like to share?
Alex: Thanks to the Jacobi family for their friendship and giving us this opportunity, inviting us to collaborate in Tailwind's kitchen! We have met incredible people who have become part of our family and friends. We are very happy to be part of this community.

❋   ❋   ❋

SNAKE EPIPHANY

"Holy shit, that's a giant snake!" I heard the distinct shriek of a damsel in distress. Five years into my jungle life, I was leading a women's retreat group on a hike when a huge boa constrictor slithered across the path in front of us. Twelve pairs of brightly painted toenails froze behind me in terror. As their leader, I had a split second to react. The words that tumbled out of my mouth? "Look, how beautiful!" I found myself genuinely admiring the snake—healthy and sleek, with gracefully symmetrical diamonds decorating its 3-meter length. I proceeded to explain to the nervous ladies that boas are an indicator of a healthy jungle ecosystem.

I was awestruck, not only by the exquisite snake, but by my inner calm. In the past, the mere thought of reptiles had sent horrified chills from my head to toes. Given this new reaction, something deep within me had undoubtedly shifted. On that day, in February 2013 (five years after opening the lodge), my love of the jungle became *real*. I would later learn that the serpent is one of the most widespread mythological symbols, offering profound wisdom around transformation, rebirth, harmony, and healing. In some cultures, snakes are perceived as an umbilical cord, joining all humans to Mother Earth.

Aptly, on the day of that boa encounter, I embraced the wild pulse of life. I had genuinely become "The Jungle Girl," a nickname that I wear proudly to this day.

LEARNING TO READ NATURE

What brought on this shift? My once superficial relationship with the jungle had been transformed as I realized that I am *a part of* the wilderness. I no longer feared the wildlife; instead, I considered us to be on the same team.

Progressive farmers count and catalog the bird diversity around their pastures as a way of assessing the health of their farm. I wasn't yet counting the bugs and snakes in the jungle, but like these farmers, I had come to understand the vital importance of a healthy, thriving ecosystem. Fascinated, I began to observe nature and sought to *learn* from it. What I had initially perceived as a jungle cacophony was revealing itself to me as a symphony.

Many ant highways and spectacular boas have come and gone since then. We've even made peace with the *tejones*. Guests are educated upon arrival about the importance of food storage and all of our fridges and cupboards now have sturdy latches. The *tejones* have learned that if the latch is closed, they have no chance at a feast of tasty tidbits, and they simply move on. Hooray for peaceful solutions! No slingshots necessary.

MINDFULNESS PAUSE: FOREST BATHING

Shinrin yoku is a Japanese term directly translated as nature bathing or nature therapy. It is defined as the act of letting nature into your body through all five senses. Florence Williams, author of *The Nature Fix*, illuminates forest bathing as a powerful tool for healing and balancing the mind and body. She offers the following guidelines.

1. **Find a spot.** Make sure you have left your phone and camera behind. You are going to be walking aimlessly and slowly. You don't need any devices. Let your body be your guide. Listen to where it wants to take you. Follow your nose. And take your time. It doesn't matter if you don't get anywhere. You are not going anywhere. You are savoring the sounds, smells, and sights of nature and letting the forest in.

2. **Open your five senses.** Let nature enter through your ears, eyes, nose, mouth, hands, and feet. Listen to the birds singing and the breeze rustling in the leaves of the trees. Look at the different greens of the trees and the sunlight filtering through the branches. Smell the fragrance of the forest and breathe in the natural aromatherapy. Taste the freshness of the air as you take deep breaths. Place your hands on the trunk of a tree. Dip your fingers or toes in a stream. Lie on the ground. Drink in the flavor of the forest and release your sense of joy and calm. This is your sixth sense, a state of mind. Now you have connected with nature. You have crossed the bridge to happiness.

❋   ❋   ❋

There is seemingly no end to the lessons that the natural world has to teach. Each morning I wonder, *what might this new jungle day bring?* Anything is possible, and I have learned to respect, appreciate, observe, and seek guidance from the flora, fauna, and local people, too (we are all part of this unique system).

Above all, the most profound lesson that the jungle has taught me thus far is that change is the only permanent thing. Just as the trees shed their leaves each year, I'm learning to let go and surrender to natural cycles. Mother Nature is the big boss! Though it's important to have plans, hopes, and dreams, we are *all* at her mercy. As a friend told me recently: "Life is like a river. You must go with the flow, but don't forget to use your paddle to steer!"

MELISSA GOODWIN, GIRLGOTTAHIKE

Connecting women with nature, confidence, and camaraderie.
"I always come home thinking more clearly after some time spent out on trail."

Is this work your passion?
I am very passionate about getting more women into the outdoors and away from the stresses of a busy city/family/work life. It is too easy to stay inside, tied to our devices and our routines. By purposely making the time to get away, breathe in fresh air and have in-person conversations with others, we can begin to feel more connected to ourselves and to one another.

What do you wish you'd known prior to getting started?
That in the beginning, learning about your business is more important than turning a profit from it. Starting a business takes a huge investment of money and of time. Though it's natural to want to start making that back immediately, there is a great deal of value in testing out your business model and in learning from your experiences before charging (or charging much) for your services. By taking people out on hikes for free, I was able to hone in what I needed to do to prepare both myself and my clients for future trips, without the pressure of feeling like the whole experience had to be perfect from the start.

Advice?

Stop thinking about it and just begin. Having an action plan is a good thing, but you don't have to have all the details worked out ahead of time to start. As you work on your business, it will naturally develop and change over time as you hone in on what it is you are offering. If possible, keep other income streams coming in before you make the leap full time into your own business. You can always start slowly with it—build it on nights and weekends or set aside a few hours a week outside of your other obligations. If you begin to rely financially on what you are super passionate about before you get some of the kinks worked out, you may end up resenting what you began or forgetting the true reasons behind what got you excited about it in the first place.

❋　❋　❋

BIOMIMICRY—THE GENIUS OF NATURE

Following these natural epiphanies, the term "biomimicry" flickered onto my radar. This philosophy encourages us to solve problems by asking the question, "How would nature do this?" This concept hadn't meant much to me in a classroom at Middlebury College, but now that I had a business in the jungle, I was intrigued.

Biomimicry seeks sustainable solutions to human challenges by emulating nature's time-tested patterns and strategies. It's a bridge between biology and design. "When we stare . . . deeply into nature's eyes, it takes our breath away, and in a good way, it bursts our bubble. We realize that all our inventions have already appeared in nature in a more elegant form and at a lot less cost to the planet," writes Janine Benyus, in her book *Biomimicry*. "The natural world has countless models for sustainable systems—prairies, coral reefs, old-growth redwood, and more. It's an encyclopedia of knowledge, experience, efficiency, and function. If we want to build a pump, let's look at the most powerful pumps on the planet—whale hearts. Even the wheel, which we always took to be a uniquely human creation, has been found in the tiny rotary motor that propels the flagellum of the world's most ancient bacteria."

When it comes to designing our wild businesses, why not use the natural world as a source of information and wisdom? Many ecosystems are doing what we want to do, but in a way that exists gracefully on this planet. Clearly, the natural world has a 3.8-billion-year head start with its designs (we have some catching up to do), but early inventors such as the Wright brothers and their winged contraptions have led the way as some of the first biomimics. Other simple inventions such as fishing nets were likely inspired by the web of spiders. Simple, yet profoundly transformative, right?

A TRUE BIOMIMIC

Dear friend of mine and plant whisperer Britta Jankay established her organic farm just outside of San Pancho. Her succulent, nutrient-rich veggies have made her somewhat of a local celebrity among gringos and Mexicans alike. The line at her farmers-market stand is long, and well worth the wait. Britta's vibrant greens grace my plate daily, yum!

Britta doesn't just grow plants. She has a deep *relationship* with her garden, formally called Ranchito Del Mar, but which I've fondly nicknamed "Britta's Secret Garden." It is fascinating to watch her listen to and study her plants. Her energy is calm, grounded, graceful, and flowing. She says: "Nature teaches me so much. I love going to the garden each day and finding new surprises. Each plant has its own rhythm, yet they all work together." She explains that gardening is a process of observing. You can't speed up anything; you can't control anything. You can only guide the garden and support it. "I do as much planning as I can, but the rest is up to nature."

When it comes to Wildpreneurship, Britta may be ahead of the game. An article by Lisa Gates in *Forbes Magazine*, "Could Biomimicry Be the Key to Negotiating Your Startup's Success?" recommends that young businesses look to nature for advice, and for competitive advantage. In my jungle experience, I wholeheartedly agree. Nature has been an infinite source of wisdom that has been good for my business *and* my bank account. Eco-friendly business decisions can make financial sense and are an effective way to win customers (people are demanding more green businesses and creative eco-solutions).

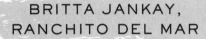

BRITTA JANKAY, RANCHITO DEL MAR

Organic farmer and biomimic.
*"Each year, things are flowing more easily.
My garden and I grow in different ways."*

Where do you find inspiration? How do you keep yourself motivated?
Seeing how beautiful all the crops grow from seed to harvest, and upstanding growing cycles and that everything has its timing, you cannot slow down or speed up any process. Nature knows what she is doing; you just have to work with her. She does amazing things! I am motivated by the people who buy my greens. They are so grateful and happy to have them, this is very satisfying.

Describe your perfect day of work and play.
Jungle run, swim in the ocean, nice breakfast, relax. Head to the garden and harvest until sunset to prepare for market the next morning. So fulfilling.

What's your favorite part about being a Wildpreneur?
Managing my own time, making my own decisions, not depending on others.

✳   ✳   ✳

BECOMING A BIOMIMIC

How can you integrate biomimicry into your wild business? Becoming a biomimic means transitioning from learning about nature to learning from nature. Wildpreneurs look to the natural world with a beginner's mind, just as we would look to our mentors and teachers. From there, we can use nature's systems as models, springboards for our creativity. As we proceed, the fundamental question we must pose alongside each decision we make is "Will this allow life to continue?" The Biomimicry Institute[28] also offers ten "Life's Principles" to guide designs and systems, outlined below.

At the Tailwind Jungle Lodge, we are consistently working to incorporate these principles into our designs. Some efforts have been straightforward, some not so much. As in the natural world, the lodge is ever changing, evolving, adapting, learning, and improving. I've briefly broken down our experience with biomimicry as a resource for Wildpreneurs, but remember that perfection is not the goal here. Nature is perfectly imperfect!

1. Nature uses only the energy it needs and relies on freely available energy. Passive solar cooling (open air structures are cooled by the breeze, no AC), an extensive gravity-fed water system (no pumps necessary), energy efficient appliances, and minimal lighting (candles offer lovely ambience) have been highly effective and practical. When the power goes out, many of our guests barely notice. What energy is available to power your business?

Living aboard Swell (sailboat) has allowed me to drastically reduce my daily impact on the earth. Solar and wind power provide my electricity. I live closer to nature, and take time to cherish and appreciate it. I use less, need less, and want less—yet have never felt more fulfilled.

—CAPTAIN LIZ CLARK

2. Nature recycles *everything*. The natural world can't put its factory on the edge of town. Research the recycling and composting opportunities in your area, but don't stop at that, there are countless creative ways to go beyond this. At the lodge, we focus on natural building materials, minimal packaging, reuse, composting toilets, and more. What can you do to minimize and recycle your waste? Keep in mind that some of the greatest opportunities in the twenty-first century may be turning waste into profit. Is there potential for that within your business?

3. Nature is resilient. Where a tree falls in the jungle, new life immediately springs up. What can you do to create diversity and cooperation within your wild business so it will be prepared to bounce back quickly? Don't just plant one crop, go for a mosaic that works together.

4. Nature optimizes rather than maximizes. Be mindful of your limits—personally, environmentally, and financially. Consider a baby whale or the sapling of a redwood tree; they start tiny and grow slowly until they reach their optimal shape/size. Nature is attuned to the power of a slow and steady approach and sustainable parameters.

NATACHA RADOJEVIC, MOANA SURF LIFE

Surf retreats, expeditions, and boutique.

Your favorite part about life as a Wildpreneur?
Being out there in the ocean with passing turtles and wildlife. It makes me feel like I am part of something magical. Nature for me is what reenergizes, heals, and inspires me. I can never get enough of Mother Nature—she fills my soul and heart with so much joy.

Advice?
Listen to your heart and natural instinct; your intuition always knows best. You may fail at first but some dreams take a little

more time to attain. Never give up if it's what makes you truly happy and fulfilled. Your life is compiled of memories, and those are what you are left with at the end of the day. What makes you truly happy will make this a better world.

*　　*　　*

5. Nature rewards cooperation. "Though there is plenty of predation, parasitism, and competition in the natural world, prevailing relationships are cooperative," says Benyus. Most animals travel in flocks, gaggles, schools, and prides. Packs offer strength, safety, and competence. At the Tailwind Jungle Lodge, we synergize as a family (the Jacobi pack!), with our neighbors, and the local community. How might you and your business collaborate and synergize?

6. Nature runs on information. Weather, tide, wind, and swells— natural sources of information that alert and prompt us to prepare accordingly. How can you be mindful of the natural cycles in your surrounding environment?

MIKE WOOD, SUSALMON, ALASKA

Low-volume, high-quality, fisherman-direct salmon business, with a focus on raising awareness of the Susitna watershed.
"My passion is for this place and all its wildness. My motivation is to be immersed in all it has to offer every day. This land is a wild teacher."

Describe your perfect day as a Wildpreneur.
When it all comes together. Wind, weather, tide, fish, and crew. It's long and tiring and you get to go at it again tomorrow.

Advice?
Be open to advice, but follow your gut. Tomorrow's businesses

don't look like the past. Especially when we have to learn to make more from less and add value to a priceless commodity.

What is your mission?
To inspire love for the mighty Susitna River and get people to care one delicious salmon at a time. I firmly believe that if people know where their food comes from, they'll pay way more attention to protecting that place, and that's what this is all about. We aim to win their hearts through their stomachs!

Source: salmonlife.org,
"The River at the Heart of It"

✹   ✹   ✹

7. **Nature uses chemistry and materials that are safe for living beings.** We just love Dr. Bronner's peppermint soap tingle, particularly because it's jungle friendly. How can you integrate natural products into your business?

8. **Nature uses abundant resources.** We have a unique type of tree here that my parents nicknamed "lover trees." A fig embraces a palm tree, as though frozen in an eternal embrace. The locals call these *higueras*, or strangler figs in English. (It's actually a parasitic relationship, the fig eventually kills the palm. Sorry, romantics.) Several of these spectacular trees fell on our property, and we used them as posts to support *palapa* roofs. What resources are abundant in your area?

KATIE AND SPENCER GRAVES, EATERY 66

Farm to trailer, local cuisine in an Airstream.
Motto: Be Good. Live Simple. Eat Well.

What was your inspiration to create Eatery 66?

Our inspiration was drawn from the farmers and ranchers of the local community. Living in Costa Rica for eight years, we strongly supported a sustainable lifestyle where we ate according to season, food availability, and local sourcing. We ate mangos off the trees, fish from the waters right out our doors, and vegetables grown within the country. Moving to Southwest Colorado, we found this same beautiful community here!

When we started Eatery 66, we wanted to create a platform to showcase the amazing local food grown and raised in the area and highlight the family who make this possible for us all. We love to inspire and educate others on the sustainability of local and organic foods through simple cuisine that allows the food to speak for itself. We have a deep passion to pave the way in this area to support and highlight our local farms and ranches, inspiring a more sustainable future for our community and beyond.

Advice?

Don't force things. When something isn't proving to work as you had initially planned, take a step back and allow for the next option to be brought forth. From something as small as furniture choices to liquor licenses, allow your business to unfold naturally. Follow your vision, but allow for there to be passages to explore the possibilities that you didn't plan/see/envision/expect! Open yourself to the growth of change and be willing to evolve.

Your favorite part?

The freedom to create. This drives us. As we develop our businesses, being stale or stagnant isn't an option. We thrive on the creative forces of newness and exploration of possibilities. We love that we can try new things, find new passions, and create a lifestyle that works for our employees and our family. For example, we take time off when we need to recharge and reboot ourselves, our staff, and our space—to clear the way for positive new energy and a break from the mundane.

Anything else to share?
We are beyond grateful for this path to grow and learn each day, with one another, with a supportive and beautiful community, all the while enjoying our lifestyle motto: "From Mountains to Oceans."

Family means the world to us. We love our three boys—Cole, Ollie, and Tristan—to the moon, and this ride is nothing without them. They bring us so much joy and are a true part of our adventure. We are also very grateful to a beautiful team of committed and dedicated employees who are more like an extended family to us.

Finally, balance is everything—work hard, play hard, rest well. Find balance and find sweetness in the little moments; the journey is only beautiful if you take a moment to breath it all in.

✻ ✻ ✻

9. **Nature works locally.** We are proud of our community and make localism a priority: employees, supplies, events, fundraisers, nonprofits, and so on. Our community center—Entreamigos (EA)[29]—has played a tremendous role in uniting expats, locals, and tourists. The founder of EA, Nicole Swedlow, received an award from the Dalai Lama in 2014, recognizing her as an "Unsung Hero of Compassion." How can you practice localism and get involved with your community?

10. **Nature uses shape to determine functionality.** The steep slope of our land has allowed us to incorporate gravity-fed water systems while the orientation and cool breeze that funnels up the ravine allows for passive solar cooling. Observe your canvas. How can you use shape to improve the functionality of your business?

MY EVOLUTION

Biomimicry is actually just one of many philosophies that have fueled my desire to marry nature and business. In college, I merged two departments to create a personalized major I called "Environmental Economics." Subsequently, internships in Colorado with Natural Capitalism Solutions and Sustainable Travel International (STI) guided my thought process. STI supported me through the arduous process of achieving a sustainability certification for the Tailwind Jungle Lodge. In 2009, the Tailwind Jungle Lodge became the first certified eco-lodge in Mexico (through STI). This earned us accolades in the ecotourism industry and continued to stoke my interest in sustainable business systems.

NICOLE SWEDLOW, ENTREAMIGOS COMMUNITY CENTER

**Social Wildpreneur, Unsung Hero of
Compassion Award from the Dalai Lama.**
*"I love the ability to live fully in this world. I get to spend
my entire day immersed in work and a life that I care about.
It is a wild life, but a special one, and I would never trade it out."*

Describe your early vision/inspiration.
I fell in love with the simplicity and sweet international community of San Pancho. However, things were starting to change as this little village was becoming "discovered," mostly by older retired American and Canadian expats. These new arrivals were great people and really respectful of the town, however, many were overwhelmed by the language barrier and "didn't want to change things." What many of them didn't realize is that just by being there, building their homes, and spending time in the community, they were changing things. Thus, I created a community center that valued everyone (locals and ex-

pats) and all contributions. I wanted to be realistic and find a win-win for this growing community.

Is this work your passion?
Yes, Entreamigos is and has been my lifework. I discovered a place where I could have the liberty to express all of my love for the world, all of my creativity, and all of my commitment. I love to rise to the challenge of each day, to create a new solution—it is my inspiration. There will never be enough space in this world to express the gratitude that I have for having been gifted the experience of Entreamigos.

What advice would you give to a potential Wildpreneur?
Just start. Find your passion and start doing it in little tiny pieces. I think that we get caught up in media reports of these over-the-top amazingly successful people, and we think that we have to have it all together before we even start. The truth is that life goes fast and very few people will ever have it all together. Living your passion is a gift, so if you can give it to yourself in tiny chunks at first, it's still a gift that you are giving . . . and no worries, you'll fall so in love with what you are doing that you will find ways to make it grow optimally.

❋   ❋   ❋

CONFUSION

Yet, despite my extensive experiences with sustainability theory and practice, I often found myself scratching my head in bewilderment as I grappled with the question: What is a sustainable business? Ridiculously complex, that's what it is. The more I learned, the more confused I became. Loaded with nuances and conflicting philosophies, sustainability is far from clear.

As we developed the lodge, I ran into countless sustainability conundrums. Do we buy hardwood chairs from sustainably forested rainforests in South America in order to protect the jungle and hardwoods of Mexico? I did my best to navigate these challenges but often felt exasperated by competing demands between environment, economy, and community.

Realistically, when it comes to sustainability, there is no right answer. Progressive free thinkers have actually tossed the term "sustainability" out of their vocabulary. However, there are many theories that shouldn't be negated: triple bottom line (economy, community, ecology), conscious capitalism, natural capitalism, social responsibility, and, of course, biomimicry just to name a few.

Why decide on one approach? Let's add a holistic twist! As we blaze our own trails, Wildpreneurs aspire to environmental, social, economic, and personal health. Let's look beyond exploitive, high stress, and damaging businesses. We have the opportunity to take the good from traditional capitalism, and embrace a new model that hinges upon collaboration, synergies, experimentation, and creativity that jives with natural systems. Let's create genuinely *good* businesses—good for ourselves and all aspects of the world around us. Wildpreneurs can make it happen.

DARRIN POLISCHUK, EVOLOVE MEDIA AND PRODUCTION

Motto: Love of life and the story.

What are you working on now?
My new production company, EvoLove, is a reincarnation of the things that are important to me, a continuation of my exit from big corporate TV. I worked with Fox TV in California for many years producing action sports programs. I encountered a crisis of conscience when I realized that the sponsors of my shows were the sugary drink, video game, and oil companies. I requested that a couple of the 30-second commercials during my

show be gifted to an NGO [nongovernmental organization], and I received a big NO, so I cancelled my contract and headed to Mexico—time for a value realignment. I wasn't fulfilled, not even close!

From there, I was tempted to head off to be an ecoterrorist, hah! But my Mexico life lead me to surf, start a family, create a variety of wild businesses, and eventually launch EvoLove. EvoLove is truly the culmination of a lifetime of random, Wildpreneur pursuits (I wrote a mountain biking guide to British Columbia, sold T-shirts out of an Airstream trailer, and worked extensively in all aspects of film and production). EvoLove brings it all together with a holistic approach to videography/ short promo films. Our clients are companies that truly want to make a difference. My work gives me complete creative freedom and a way to give back. My mission is to connect ocean, health, nature, movement, love, people, community, and planet. I feel driven to close the loop of business and to create a synergy of holistic, conscious businesses. Right now, I'm working on a promotional video and experiential event for a gala fundraiser to raise money for victims of Hurricane Willa.

Advice?
You don't have to study your trade formally. To get started with filmmaking, I rented cameras and learned from mentors. I figured out how to look behind the "magic curtain" of what's on the surface to find the real story, then I just put it out there.

On natural rhythms . . .
My business works with seasonal rhythms—there is a significant ebb and flow. Winter is high tourist season—time for doing, getting out there, connecting, and collaborating. Summer is hot, humid, rainy season—time for hibernation, getting slow, and working on personal projects. I really enjoy this cycle.

❋   ❋   ❋

FIGHTING THE CURRENT TOGETHER

As inspired, progressive thinkers, we must work together to lead the charge toward holistic business. We *need* to put words into action. This will not be an easy task, but if we don't do it, who will? As we reach our resource limits, it's high time for us to tune into the Earth's wisdom.

May we hear and embody Benyus's call to action: We must seek the eddies in the river. Eddies are pockets of calm, circulating water in a river; a magic haven in the shadow of a rock. This is a place a kayaker can duck into to rest or retreat. Benyus explains that getting your boat into an eddy is hard work, "It takes some momentum and a vigorous, well-placed paddle brace to pivot across the eddy line and into the sanity of smoother water. In the same way, our transition to sustainability must be a deliberate choice to leave the linear surge of an extractive economy and enter a circulating, renewable one."

FLEETING MOMENTS

Evenings on my jungle rooftop find me gazing out over the ocean. Pelicans cruise effortlessly in circles, gracefully riding the wind thermals. This playful display triggers Baja nostalgia, where my daydreams for the creation of the jungle lodge began.

"Watch out for the Mexican air force!" Rhett called as pelicans dive-bombed into the water beside us. I giggled happily, loving the pelicans, dolphins, turtles, whales, and stingrays that frolicked alongside our boats. Sea lions honked, crabs clicked their way around the barnacled rocks, and coyotes howled through the night. These unique creatures filled my heart with joy as I marveled at the bond that we share called "life."

EXCERPT FROM POEM: BIOMIMICRY BECKONS US TO GROW UP

By Yael Flusberg, yoga teacher

A blanket of sawdust on the pillows
by the bay windows, the only remnant
of a great oak felled after a botched trim
metastasized inside. Now we're all exposed.

Nature doesn't always win, but we can learn
from her losses. We could grab water out of fog,
learn from carnivorous plants
in bogs how to attract what we need.

The receptive principle is not slash and burn
and mine down to the core. It's waiting.
It's watching what has risen to the surface.
For today, it's enough to stay still.

✻   ✻   ✻

CHAPTER SIX

SIMPLIFICATION & ADAPTATION— IS IT MAÑANA YET?

MY BIGGEST CHALLENGE AS A WILDPRENEUR HAS BEEN LEARNING TO ADAPT TO THE MEXICAN MINDSET, WHICH ONCE YOU UNDERSTAND IT (IF YOU ARE FORTUNATE ENOUGH TO DO SO), MAKES PERFECT SENSE. —EL TIGRE

WILDPRENEUR TRAIL MAP #6

The lessons in this section are particularly valuable to Wildpreneurs living and working internationally. However, regardless of location, a willingness to be flexible is an invaluable asset to the longevity of your business. Adaptation is crucial for navigating the unknown. In this chapter you will discover:

- The need for personal and professional adaptation.
- Your ability to learn from and flow with the culture that surrounds you (crucial!).
- The simple wisdom of the Mexican fisherman.
- Change and challenge are inevitable; struggle is optional.

✳   ✳   ✳

If the human body replaces itself with newly generated cells every seven to ten years, then my Canadian/American cells are becoming Mexican. In the last decade, my DNA has been infused with chili peppers and tequila; Latin culture has certainly added spice to my life. Yet, at the beginning of my jungle journey, my speedy, productivity-driven cells resisted change with all their might. As I struggled, I eventually realized that in order to survive in this new place, I needed to adapt—personally and professionally.

As the Mexican culture now flows through my veins, I've come to see the world through a whole new lens. The rigid, horn-rimmed spectacles I wore in college are long gone, replaced with laidback sunglasses. As the framework of my life shifted, my perception of what matters most in life has been transformed as well.

TREE OF ADAPTATION

You may find it useful to think of your evolving wild life as a tree. When I first put down roots in Mexico and began to sprout our family business, I was a naive little sapling. The roots and trunk of my tree of adaptation began with my understanding of Mexican culture. This was followed by two branches of adaptation: personal and professional. Though my initial intention had been for the branches of my business to grow rapidly and steadily upward, with the sky as the limit, this wasn't meant to be. If I were to thrive in Mexico, I would have to abandon the notion of being like an oak or a maple with dozens of branches and thousands of leaves. Instead, I became a palm tree with a few sturdy fronds that bend and sway in the tropical breeze.

CARPE DIEM—MAÑANA?

My story of adaptation truly began with the word "mañana." This famous adverb has two direct translations. It can mean "tomorrow;" it can also mean "morning." Which is it? The ambiguity seems to be intentional. Herein lies the beginning of the Mexican cultural paradox.

My expat friends have similar versions of how they came to understand this cornerstone of Mexican culture (and different variations of the "mañana culture" throughout the world). My mañana education began when we ran into our first plumbing issues in the jungle in 2008. I called Tulo Garcia, son of our builder, Adalberto. Tulo happily reassured me over the phone "*Si, si, si,*" he'd come fix the toilet "mañana." I assumed he meant tomorrow morning, but tomorrow morning came and went with no sign of Tulo. I dialed him *again*.

"*Si, si,* Tamara, *no te preoccupes, voy*!" (don't worry, I'm coming) or "*llego en un momentito*!" (I'll arrive in a minute!).

Thus, I would wait. And wait. And wait. In the United States, I would have called another plumber/electrician, but given Tulo's monopoly on plumbing/electrical work in the jungle, he was the only game in town.

As I waited, a spectrum of emotions marched through me: patience transitioned to annoyance, that turned to extreme frustration, which gave way to anger and despair. When Tulo finally arrived (days later), I was so grateful that my waiting was over that I hugged him enthusiastically, and we did a happy little dance—all angst forgotten.

Tulo would dive into his work smiling, whistling, singing, and making silly animal noises. He seemed to enjoy his work even when unclogging a shower drain or fixing my septic system. I watched him scratch his head at puzzles—boiling hot water in the toilets, root systems strangling our water lines and other such mysteries—and refuse to give up until he'd solved the problem.

But with his mastery came my vexation—oh, how he has made me wait! "Waiting for Tulo" has actually become a family saying that we use whenever we're expecting someone who is running late. Like Tulo, many Mexicans seem to live in their own time zone. Don't be surprised if you, too, find yourself "waiting for Tulo," particularly if you chose to live and work in a developing country. Punctuality and speedy service are not necessarily a global standard or objective.

Tulo was the merciless beginning to my cultural education. He stretched the ambiguity of the word "mañana" as far as it would go. But Tulo continued to remind me: "*No te preoccupes*, Tamara, *voy*" (Don't worry, I will be there [eventually]).

I scratched my head, befuddled by this and other bizarre Mexican idiosyncrasies. While everyone is waiting for mañana to come, they're busy making crazy noises, just like Tulo! Next to tardiness, unnecessary noise used to make the hair stand up on the back of my neck. In the classic book, *God and Mr. Gomez*, Jack C. Smith[30] describes a Mexican morning:

> The roosters crow; first one tentative voice, then another, and finally the entire town is aroused and crowing. Then the bells begin to ring . . . and finally the radios come on in every house and hovel, crowding the morning air with a chaos of lively Mexican music and commercials delivered in rapid fire Spanish like bulletins of disaster.

This culture was late and noisy. What had I gotten myself into? Clearly, I was not assimilating well. I was the yin to the Mexican yang. I steadfastly adhered to my to-do list and strict agenda with impatient steam coming out of my ears as I waited for workers and service providers. I jammed on headphones in an attempt to block out the frenzy of noise in town. As I clung to my values of productivity, growth, punctuality, and organization, I was miserable.

CULTURE SHOCK

A year into the creation of the lodge, I was in culture shock, homesick for what I'd left behind. I yearned for Middlebury—the quiet, manicured campus and predictable, structured schedule. I missed English speakers! I longed for kale, drinking water out of the tap, and putting toilet paper in the toilet. This culture shock was a factor that I hadn't considered in my daydreams of starting the lodge. You may also feel like a fish out of water as you plunge into a new environment, community, and a new business. Don't be surprised if you feel homesick in a variety of ways. If you left behind a desk job and paycheck, you might even miss that, too. The grass is always greener on the other side of the fence. Practice patience—this new journey will require a period of adjustment.

American expats around the world can relate to this sentiment. Writer Mark Manson, author of *The Subtle Art of Not Giving a F*ck*, explains that in his experiences abroad, there are three phases of expat living.[31] The first phase is missing the comforts and conveniences of home. Check. I had all the symptoms.

SPEED BUMPS

The speed bumps snapped me out of it. I would have been stuck on phase one for a lot longer had it not been for the ubiquitous *topes* (speed bumps) on the roads. These unmarked concrete monsters force you to hit the brakes and pause. There is simply no avoiding them. As I summited the peak of my millionth *tope* (sometime during my second year of living in Mexico), my annoyance fizzled and expired, replaced with acceptance and surrender. The iron will of "Turbo Tam" had been broken by the mañana culture. I was exhausted. Resisting the culture around you is energy wasted. Open your mind and your heart.

With this realization, the lines of frustration on my face relaxed and my eyes opened wide to Mexico for the first time. Oh, Mexico, the land of fiestas and siestas, where homemade fresh corn tortillas are eaten at every meal. Streets are filled with brilliant colors, an array of smells, and vibrant life. Kids play everywhere and parenting is a community effort. Women teeter around in bedazzled high-heeled shoes on cobblestone streets (it's an impressive balancing act). Hoop earrings and tight jeans are always in style here, and curves are celebrated. Cowboys and mariachis in sequined outfits hang out together sipping cervezas (beer) and playing dominoes on the corner. Speed bumps (*topes*) and soccer balls are everywhere, as are telenovelas (melodramatic Latin American TV shows) that play on dusty old TVs in *tiendas* (small stores), fruit stands, and homes alike. The word "adios" can be used to say hello or goodbye, and, really, what's the difference? There's always time to sip a coconut and have a chat. My observations of this lively culture are clearly broad generalizations to be sure, but when you wander down the street of a traditional Mexican village, I bet that you'll spot at least one of these things. What might you expect to see in the culture around you?

PERSONAL ADAPTATION

As I slowed down and observed the culture, a strange thing happened. Amid the chaos I discovered the charm. I entered into phase two of expat living: I opened my heart to this new culture. If you can't beat 'em, join 'em, right? I made the decision to adapt. You, too, will have to make that choice, whether you're in the United States or abroad. Humans are continually adapting to the changing world around them. Your brain is naturally inclined to adapt, but you have to let it—it's OK to step gently out of your comfort zone. In fact, it's a very healthy habit to cultivate as a Wildpreneur. "You have to morph to be successful, people rarely get it all right on the first attempt. You have to be open to change and move as your intuition and vision show you how," says Wildpreneur Shannon Hughes, founder of Terra-Mar Realty.

I loosened my grip on my rigid agenda and lengthy to-do list. I no longer looked down my nose in disdain at those taking siestas in hammocks. Instead, I strung up my own hammock and declared it my "no stresspassing zone." Though it felt strange to trade relentless productivity for hammock time, I soon got the hang of it. Go ahead, sample the local culture.

When we invited some local kids to the jungle one day to paint signs for our interpretive natural trail, I was captivated by their joy and delight in the simple things. They returned my curiosity as they asked me about where I'd come from and who I was. As I opened my heart to the community and the people, they opened their hearts to me. Suddenly, I was eager to understand Mexican culture.

This would be no easy task. Truly adapting to Mexican culture would mean rewiring my brain. Organization, professionalism, and punctuality were part of my personality (I'm the kind of person who has nightmares about running late for school). So, I resolved to watch, learn, and put myself in a Mexican's shoes. I often felt like I was driving on the beach as I consistently got stuck. I would spin my wheels with all my might, but only dig myself a deeper hole of frustration. My only way forward was to embrace a new approach. It wasn't until a guest of mine told me the parable of the Mexican fisherman that everything suddenly clicked into four-wheel drive.

TARA GIMMER, HEADSHOT PHOTOGRAPHER

Mobile headshot studio in an Airstream trailer.

Advice?
Have a plan.
Be open to adapting your plan.
Your life evolves.
Listen to what your life tells you.
Look for synchronicities!

What do you love about being a Wildpreneur?
Being able to live anywhere I want as long as there is an airport and internet.

THE PARABLE OF THE MEXICAN FISHERMAN

The following is my version of the parable of the Mexican fisherman (originally written by German writer Heinrich Böll):[32]

An American businessman was vacationing in a Mexican village when a small fishing boat landed on the beach. A whistling fisherman hoped onto the sand and unloaded several mahi mahi (dorado). Impressed, the American asked the fisherman how long he'd been out on the water.

The Mexican looked up from beneath his sombrero, smiled, and replied: "Only a few hours. I catch what I need—a couple for my family to eat, a couple for my friends, and a few to sell—then I head home for siesta." The American scratched his head. "But what do you do with the rest of your day?"

The fisherman responded, "I surf with my kids, lounge in the hammock, sip tequila, dance with my wife, then play guitar and dominoes with my amigos. Oh sí, señor, I have a rich and beautiful life."

The American raised his eyebrows, "Well, you know, I'm a business consultant, and I'd be happy to advise you. If you spend more time fishing you could buy a bigger boat. Then you could catch more fish and maybe even have a whole fleet of boats! Then, you could open your own fish market and your own cannery. You would control everything! You could leave this little village and move to the city where you will run your growing business."

"How long would this take?" the fisherman inquired.

"Fifteen to twenty years," the American responded.

"And then?" asked the Mexican, eyes wide.

"Well, when the time is right, you would sell your company and become very rich."

"Rich?" the fisherman responded with a dubious chuckle.

"Yes!" the American said, "Then you would retire. Move to a small fishing village where you would surf with your kids, lounge in the hammock, sip tequila, dance with your wife, then play guitar and dominoes with your amigos . . ."

FISHERMEN EVERYWHERE

I fell in love with this little story. Once I'd heard it, I saw different versions of it all around me. My employees and helpers in the jungle (maids, construction workers, chefs, gardeners), the businesses in town, my Mexican amigos—all seemed to be distant relatives of the fisherman. I finally understood Tulo, the master of getting slow. An expert at his trade, he deliberately takes his time solving the mysteries of jungle plumbing and electricity. He finds the joy in each moment, whatever he may be doing. He prioritizes family and quality of life above work.

As the fisherman story deepened my understanding of traditional Mexican culture, it also reiterated the wisdom of "less is more," and reinforced my values of family, play, purpose, conscious living, and simplicity—personally and professionally. I was also more certain than ever that I didn't want to wait to start living my life. For me, success would be quality of life, not necessarily the numbers in my bank account.

WHAT KIND OF FISHERMAN ARE YOU? ♥

Grab your timer and set it for 20 minutes. As you design your life, consider your personal values and the big picture of your life:

- What are your values?
- What is your ideal balance of work and play?
- What does your ideal lifestyle look like?
- What does happiness mean to you?
- What are your priorities? Family? Work? Leisure?
- What is enough? We've visited this before; this fundamental question should be considered frequently!

✳   ✳   ✳

BECOMING MEXICAN

When I finally received my Mexican green card in 2013, declaring me a permanent resident of Mexico, I was proud and grateful. This benchmark went beyond a piece of paper. I felt like a Mexican! I was surprised and excited by my personal transformation. Mexico had prompted me to recalibrate my core values and life as a whole. A. J. Jacobs, author and editor of *Esquire* magazine, says, "I had always thought you change your mind and you change your behavior, but it's often the other way around, you change your behavior and you change your mind." There was no doubt that living in Mexico had changed the way I think. How might living in a new culture change you? Might the unfamiliar become familiar? And loved by you?

Rick Kahn, a fellow Wildpreneur, downsized his life and sought simplicity in San Pancho. He stepped away from his all-consuming career, sold his large Victorian home in Boulder, Colorado, and squeezed everything he could fit into his old Toyota 4-Runner. He says that his extreme action "freaked a lot of people out," but he felt liberated as he drove south to design his new life and career. He now works as a business coach and describes his perfect day in San Pancho as "Surf early; catch the sunrise from the water, a few friends to enjoy it with; solar shower from a liter bottle cooked on the dashboard, then dive into a few coaching calls, or a volunteer project. Ceviche for lunch, freshly made, a hike, walk on the beach, bike ride, or even a siesta, practice a little guitar or ukulele, then find a spot for sunset and dinner with friends—simplicity."

Though Rick had a privileged approach to simplicity (investments, savings, etc.) and was focused on downsizing, there are different ways to design your life around simplicity. Many Wildpreneurs have opened small, simple businesses with very little capital, a dash of creativity and resourcefulness, as we discovered in chapter 3.

RICK KAHN, EXECUTIVE COACH AND TRAINER

"I like to think of myself as an economic refugee who took the moment of crisis and turned it into opportunity . . . the unknown is the best teacher."

Has your business adapted/evolved over the last decade?
Absolutely. I never imagined I would be working in the capacity I am today. The single most significant influence was letting go of "making money" and being more in service. This allowed me to hone new skills without the pressure of ROI (return on investment) in terms of money. I found that the more I gave, for giving sake, the more it was appreciated. I felt incredibly encouraged to keep raising the bar for myself, reading, studying, testing, and applying new skills. The value of time became important to me, time to develop, not rush.

What are some of the challenges you've encountered as a Wildpreneur?
There is no paycheck without some creative effort; no "just showing up," cause there's no place to show up unless you're cultivating your own garden—physically, emotionally, and spiritually.

Anything else you'd like to share?
Stay in gratitude. Sure, things go wrong, get hard, and you even fail; but gratitude trumps the bumps and opens the heart and mind to possibilities.

✳   ✳   ✳

PROFESSIONAL ADAPTATION

My newfound willingness to adapt may have been my true birth as a Wildpreneur. This personal shift triggered a ripple effect throughout the branches of my life professionally. Adaptation is crucial for navigating the unknown. Yes, it's a bit ironic that I am now thanking the "mañana" culture, known for its lack of work ethic, for making my business stronger. I, too, have become a Mexican paradox.

A willingness to adapt will make your business more resilient and better equipped to navigate the speed bumps you will inevitably encounter. Furthermore, adaptation goes hand in hand with change. You may find yourself resistant to change, but don't fear it. Change may bring highs and lows, but embrace the journey, call upon your grit when you need it, and you *will* keep your dream alive. You're not adapting to cope, you're adapting to thrive.

Adaptation for your business may take many forms. The adaptations of the Tailwind Jungle Lodge over the years have been countless as we've adjusted, rearranged, renovated, and tweaked the business to adapt to changing customer needs, environment, technology, competition, industry, and other factors. Whether you're launching your business in the United States or abroad, you may learn from our experience. We've adapted to:

Needs of our customers/guests. We host a range of guests: couples, solo travelers, families, birthdays, anniversaries, weddings, yoga retreats, fitness retreats, meditation retreats, Americans, Mexicans, Canadians, retirees, backpackers, professionals, adventurers, and more. Needs vary, and we do our best to please and adapt accordingly.

Environmental challenges. We are continually adapting to the natural cycles of our surrounding environment and resources.

Changing professional goals. As the ecotourism industry exploded in this area, we had to decide: Would we grow with it? Should we? Did we want to? Once we'd reached capacity for sixteen guests, we paused and determined that we'd found our sweet spot where we optimized work and play. We were busy, but not *too* busy. Instead of expanding the lodge further, we focused on quality. Micro business suited us just fine.

Note: Your ratio of work/play may be different. Everyone is unique! You may also find that the lines between work and play become blurred, particularly if you're working in a job that fulfills you. Meaningful work isn't always just about a paycheck. It's important to keep checking in with yourself. Find the version of the fisherman parable that works for you. The world needs fishermen, but there's a place for big business and philanthropy, too

Competition. As many hotels and vacation rentals have sprung up in our area, competition is prevalent. This has actually made us a stronger business by pushing us to develop our unique personality and brand to set ourselves apart.

Feedback. We check in with our guests regularly and receive a variety of responses, both compliments and complaints. Complaints are never easy to receive, but they surely help us improve.

Industry trends. Glamping, eco-chique, and other trends come and go. We are continually evaluating our mission and position.

Neighborhood shifts. New owners bring new dynamics.

Undoubtedly, there is more adaptation on the horizon. We're content with the lodge as it is now, but who knows what mañana might bring. Speaking of "mañana," guess who showed up early the other day? Tulo! Perhaps my Mexican amigos are adapting as well? Tulo has become a dear friend over the years. We smile, sing, whistle, fix toilets, and savor simple jungle moments together.

CHEF ALONDRA MALDONADO, *FLAVORS OF NAYARIT* (BOOK)

Motto: Cuisine is the undiscovered treasure of Mexico.

"The journey to passion is transformative, and like any transformation, it is not always fun. It has many edges, but you emerge as a new being, and from that other passions are born."

Your favorite part about life as a Wildpreneur?
The taste of victory, of having achieved my dream.

Funny examples of living on a shoestring?
Phew! I have hundreds of these stories, of sacrifices mixed with "miracles." The one that I like the most is that my car decided to break down, that is, it needed a new engine. At that time I could not afford an engine! I told the mechanic. After about 15 minutes, he called to tell me that he and his wife had decided to lend me the money for the engine AND they would lend me their car so that I could continue researching—they liked my book project!

Favorite quote?
"It's not over 'til it's over."

✳   ✳   ✳

FINAL PHASE

Mexico has undoubtedly become a home for me. However, I've reached what Mark Manson describes as the final phase of expat living: a realization that "every culture is a double-edged sword." All cultures have their pros and cons.

Though I love Mexico, there are things that I don't especially care for: litter, dangerous roads, hazy rules, drugs, corruption, perpetual disorganization. I don't dwell on these things, but they are a part of this country (of course, these challenges also exist in the United States and throughout the world). When I close the lodge in June for the summer rainy season, I am excited to cross the border into the United States. Hooray for punctuality, convenience, efficiency, organization, cleanliness, and a functional mail delivery system! I am also delighted to encounter inspiring Wildpreneurs in my travels throughout the States. However, after a summer of American living with all its techy devices, ubiquitous busyness, culture of speed, and esteem for material possessions, I yearn for the simplicity and laidback vibes of Mexico. When I head south in October, I am grateful to cross the border once again.

I'm lucky to divide my life between these countries. My newfound ability to adapt has made my international lifestyle delightfully possible. I've become a citizen of North America, or what some call "a cultural mutt." This has caused occasional identity crises for me. You, too, may feel confused as you venture into the unknown, but if you're willing to adapt, you will find your way, just as I have. In my multicultural life, I've woven the simplicity of the fisherman with the ambition of the American dream to create my own culture—the jungle girl philosophy of Wildpreneurship! I giggle at the realization that I've come to celebrate the word "mañana." It's actually become a comfort, a sort of happy place that we'll arrive at some point down the road of life. Or, as Jack Kerouac puts it in *On the Road*:[33]

> "Mañana," she said. "Everything'll be all right tomorrow, don't you think, Sal-honey, man?"
> "Sure, baby, mañana." It was always mañana. For the next week, that was all I heard—mañana, a lovely word and one that probably means heaven.

YOUR TREE

Consider your tree once again as you adapt your life and your business to the speed bumps along the path that you've chosen. What will your tree of Wildpreneurship look like? Will you be a tall pine tree that reaches up to the sky with endless possibilities? Or are you more of a Joshua tree: short, sturdy, and strong? Perhaps you're a willow, content to sway gracefully. Don't be surprised if the branches of your tree take you in some directions that you weren't expecting—mine certainly did. However, I'm eternally grateful for my palm tree of life here. I wholeheartedly believe that the branches of my tree have taken me exactly where I'm supposed to be. You may guide the growth of your tree, but trust your roots and branches to take you where you need to go.

THRIVING ON ADAPTATION

Don't be surprised if you actually find yourself thriving on the challenge of adaptation. Artist Janet Echleman, famous for her elaborate sculptures, celebrates the process of working with changing conditions. She builds sculptures that adapt to the environment around them. She says that taking each moment as it comes is what keeps her practice as an artist alive. Each project she works on has a new set of constraints, and she must find new solutions. "I have to find a solution that I just don't know yet . . . it's what makes me excited to wake up and walk into the studio."

Adaptation to perpetual change may indeed be a key component to keeping wild inspiration alive. I've often daydreamed about the possibility of creating Tailwind II, perhaps the mountain version in Colorado or British Columbia—a cold-weather complement to tropical paradise. I've come to thrive on the challenge of creation. If I ever did create a second location it certainly wouldn't be focused on growth and dollar signs, it would be about following my purpose, doing work that fulfills me, and exploring where my roots and branches might take me. Go ahead, reach for the stars, but don't be blinded by your goals and destination—gaze up at the heavens while keeping your feet firmly on the ground. Let's fully enjoy our time here on Earth while we've got it.

DONNIE RUST, *THE LOST EXECUTIVE* MAGAZINE

"Get lost in the world."

What was your inspiration to create *The Lost Executive*?
I used to tell myself that I wanted to be rich, filthy rich, a millionaire, and that this would make me happy. But I was wrong. The truth is, I'm motivated by much simpler ideas, and these are the driving force behind *The Lost Executive*.

Advice?

Planning is essential, but at the same time be prepared to throw plans away and rewrite them. You have to be determined but be able to pivot. You have to be able to work hard by working smart. Being successful isn't about being the brainiest or the biggest dreamer. You don't even have to be creative. If you have the capacity to sit down and focus on completing one task at a time, you're sorted.

Favorite motivational quote?

"Do whatever you want with your life, just do it with 100 percent."

❋   ❋   ❋

DO WHAT YOU LOVE, LOVE WHAT YOU DO

As I surf, sip tequila, and watch the sunset with my Wildpreneur amigos, I see that common threads connect us: We've created businesses that do good for ourselves, our community, and the natural world. We have grand goals, drive, and purpose, but we thrive on simplicity and a healthy balance of work and play. We ride the waves of change in our wild lives, and we support one another over the speed bumps. When we get stuck in the sand, we hop on the back bumper, jump up and down, and rally our amigos to push! It's all part of adapting to whatever adventure the day brings. We're all fishermen blessed with the spark of Wildpreneur ambition. We do what we love, and we love what we do.

JEN MCCARTHY, BLUHOUSE MARKET AND CAFÉ, VANCOUVER, CANADA

Delicious. Organic. Local.

Describe your perfect day as a Wildpreneur.

Hah! There is no perfect day. Every day is different. Just when you think, "I got this!" Boom—something lands at your feet and you are dealing with new problem-solving skills you didn't know you had. Then there are the moments when the flow is so good and all the work is coming together and the team is just humming along and all you can feel is the love that oozes through the dream you have created. In those moments, I pause and say to myself, "This is what it is all about." A perfect day is when those moments outweigh the ones where you are freaking out a little and scratching your head thinking, "How am I going to deal with that pile of #@$!."

Is this work your passion?

Yes! Leaving a twenty-five-year corporate career behind meant risking a lot of stability to step out of that comfort zone and be honest about what makes me happy. Shredding external expectations of status and taking a lifestyle step down for a spiritual step up. Working and living in alignment with my values keep me motivated. When my business is a platform of expression and creating and values in action, that is the best. As your own boss, you get to decide what you say yes to and how that supports your vision or drives the business forward. The fact that the opportunities are limitless (only bound by time and money and a sensibility to prioritize) is pretty cool.

Advice?

Building a good team takes time. They are the heart of the business. "Take care of your people and they will take care of your business." And when something toxic starts to grow in that space, cut it out like a weed before it takes root. Protect what you love!

❋   ❋   ❋

CHAPTER SEVEN

INVEST IN YOURSELF

YOU, YOURSELF, AS MUCH AS ANYBODY
IN THE ENTIRE UNIVERSE, DESERVE YOUR
LOVE AND AFFECTION. —BUDDHA[34]

INVEST IN YOURSELF

Burnout? No, thank you. Radiant health? Yes, please! Wildpreneurship hinges on quality of life. Taking care of you is an integral element that starts now. Your business bottom line is meaningless without strong human capital.[35] As you invest in your business, you must also invest in yourself—deposits into your health bank account are crucial. If you make self-care a priority, you will succeed where so many entrepreneurs have crashed. Without this piece of the puzzle, all is lost.

WILDPRENEUR
TRAIL MAP #7 ♥

This highly interactive chapter will equip you with a quiver of tools to support holistically nourishing yourself for life as a Wildpreneur. A preventative approach to wellness will spare you much grief—a stitch in time saves nine. In this chapter we will focus on:

- Primary food: nourishment beyond what you put in your mouth.
- Letting go of past health challenges and self-destructive habits.
- Visualizing your best self, setting goals and creating sustainable habits for health.
- The essence of holistic nourishment and self-care.

✳   ✳   ✳

What does it mean to invest in yourself? Healthy living is different for everyone. I'm here to get you started with listening to your body, deconstructing your bio-individuality, and figuring out what works today and throughout the journey ahead. You know the old philosophy, "you can give a hungry man a fish, or you can teach him to fish and feed him for life." Get ready to learn to fish.

NICOLAS BLEVINS, ACUPUNCTURIST IN SAN PANCHO, MEXICO

"A wild business is an extension of yourself. Do the inner work. The more healthy and balanced you are as an individual, the more successful you will be."

What have you learned from your journey?
If there is anything that I've learned with this medicine, it is that healing is not linear. I believe this is also true for business and most things in life. Any journey has moments of expansion and moments of concentration. Learning to recognize these moments and adjust accordingly leads to long-term success and stability.

Advice?

Chop off your head! Obviously, you need to plan and be smart, but to succeed in a wild business, you need to lead with your heart, with your intuition, and with inspiration. People around you may think you are being careless. But in order to succeed outside the box you need to think, feel, and act outside the box. Also, give yourself the freedom to measure success in different ways. Being a Wildpreneur is not just about the money.

What is your favorite part of being a Wildpreneur?

Given the definition of Wildpreneur, I would have to say that my favorite part of being one is realizing I am one.

❋　　❋　　❋

SHANTI'S STORY—SCAR, A LOVE STORY

To love oneself is the beginning of a lifelong romance.

—OSCAR WILDE[36]

Allow me to introduce you to Shanti Tilling, founder of SweatPlay-Live. Shanti guides retreats, beach boot camps, move-your-asana classes, and is a personal trainer. She has also been an infinite source of inspiration and motivation for me personally. Shanti sports tank tops that say "I love puppies and tacos" and then leads me through the HIIT beach workouts (high-intensity interval training) that leave me covered in sand and feeling gloriously alive. When life as a Wildpreneur gets tough, there's nothing like a good sweat with Shanti and my local amigos to help me regain my balance.

Shanti's tagline is "find what moves you," and she clearly embodies this throughout her life. As a former model, her physical appearance is dazzling, but it's her inner beauty that is truly captivating. She is the epitome of balance and wellness as she radiates a contagious love of life. However, it hasn't always been that way; Shanti's health journey is a lesson for us all.

In her soulful article, titled "Scar—A Love Story,"[37] Shanti explains how, at a very young age, she was living her dream—personal training and jetting off to exotic locales with her clients all over the country and abroad. She taught fitness classes at two major film studios in the Bay Area and was a fitness model in her spare time. Yet, she writes, "While my outside looked amazing, my inside was a disgusting mess full of low self-esteem and a self-worth-ometer set at zero. I punished my body by overtraining for mountain bike races, Muay Thai (kickboxing), and trail running. Even yoga was a platform for self-abuse, beating myself up if I did not perform double *chaturangas* throughout every *vinyasa* yoga class. I now realize that I pushed my body to extremes to quiet my inner torment."

At thirty years old, her dream life came crashing down when she was diagnosed with a pancreatic tumor. Shortly after a miraculously successful surgery, she wrote in her diary: "I guess this is what people mean by getting a second chance. I am one of the lucky ones . . . I am so grateful for this chance to truly start living my life."

She reflects now, "My tumor was a self-inflicted wound created by holding in thirty years of emotional pain." Surgery left her with a scar that is a peace sign over her abdomen. Ironic, she says, "because up until that moment, I had never felt peace when it came to my stomach—shivering at the thought of being touched, and taking every opportunity to pull a shirt down. Ironic also that my name, Shanti, is Hindi for 'Peace.' I've finally accepted my body, scars and all, for what it is—mine. I now give myself permission to just be me. Instead of doing, pushing, and forcing, I feel. The truth is, we all have scars. Your scars are badges of honor. A reminder that you faced a challenge, walked through the fire, fought your demons, was presented with lessons, and survived."

HEALTHY CHANGE

Let's draw strength from Shanti's story. We all have scars, imperfections, and demons, why not own them, learn from them, and use them to make us stronger? In the words of Leonard Cohen, "There is a crack in everything. That's how the light gets in.[38] With Shanti's wisdom in mind, take a moment to reflect on your own health story, your truth. There is no ego here, no judgment. Grab your notebook, we're going to explore three elements of your health story:

- **Past.** Reflecting on your previous challenges, self-destructive habits, tendencies, and triggers will give you an idea of what you may need to work on.
- **Best you.** Focusing on times when you've felt best in your life will illuminate self-care practices that work well for you.
- **Holistic health habits.** Integrating healthy habits into your life now will make all the difference to your ability to thrive throughout your journey as a Wildpreneur.

HOW OFTEN DO YOU RECHARGE YOUR CELL PHONE?

Arianna Huffington, cofounder of The Huffington Post and author of *Thrive*, suggests treating our bodies as we do our cell phones. "We're all exquisitely aware of the recharging routine of our phones. . . . And yet, on the flipside, with our bodies and our minds and our souls, we'll run them right into the ground until they shut down."

What do you need to do to regularly recharge your batteries?

Source: Huffington Post

✳   ✳   ✳

MY STORY

I'll blaze the trail here with a quick example of reflecting on past self. I give myself permission to be me, raw and real, emotional scars and all. Here goes.

Like Shanti, my dream life came crashing down two years into the creation of my wild business. Self-destructive habits that I'd cultivated in high school (I was a victim of beauty magazines) came with me to the jungle. I struggled with anorexia, superficial obsession, and horrific cycles of binging and fasting that became my dark secret. Though I appeared fit, acne raged on my face, revealing the battle within me. Internal inflammation inevitably manifests itself externally. I felt as though the energy had been wrung out of me like a sponge squeezed dry. I had no motivation, no confidence, definitely no charm available for my guests. Though I yearned to collapse and hide, I had a business to run. I could no longer deny my health issues. Becoming a Wildpreneur may have ultimately saved my life. Might wild business push you to confront your own weaknesses and health challenges?

ACCEPTANCE, BE FLAWSOME

During my solo time in the jungle, I realized that I had a problem: I needed help. I had no idea what to eat, how to take care of myself, how to love myself. Once I was ready for help, the road to healing began. "Acceptance is the road to recovery," says Alcoholics Anonymous. I found the guidance that I craved in a program with the Institute for Integrative Nutrition. I'm delighted to pass what I've learned on to you.

Now it's your turn to share. Do any parts of my story or Shanti's resonate with you? Regardless of the severity or nature of your health challenges, let's be "flawsome" (flawed + awesome). Accepting our weaknesses and allowing ourselves to be vulnerable, raw, and real mark the true beginning of the healing process. This should come as a relief—no shame or pretending necessary.

PAST: WINDOW INTO YOUR BIO-INDIVIDUALITY♥

Grab a pen, let's invest some time in deconstructing your past self and considering your bio-individuality. At the top of the page, write: I give myself permission to be me—raw, real, scars, and all.

Take five or ten minutes to brainstorm each question. Set a timer for yourself—whether you think you're done or not, if you sit on these questions a bit, new ideas may emerge. Give yourself a chance for deeper reflection.

- What health challenges have I encountered in the past? When did they begin?
- What caused these challenges? Were they self-inflicted? Or genetic? Could they have been prevented?
- Have I resolved these issues? What did I learn from my experience? Have I consulted with a knowledgeable health practitioner?
- How is my body unique?
- More recently, how did I take care of myself yesterday? Did I make my health a priority?
- Have I had any triggers and/or deconstructive habits?

If you've been truthful in your answers and reflections, nice work! You've peeled back a layer of your onion of understanding of your unique body.

LET THAT SH*T GO EXERCISE

As my yoga teachers at the lodge say, "It's time to let that shit go!" Write down all the things that no longer serve you, then light a candle and burn that piece of paper. Repeat the mantra "release" as you go through the process. Careful, don't burn your fingers—have a bowl of water to drop the remnants into.

BEST YOU ♥

Now for the fun: When have you felt the best in your life? Take a moment to reflect and catch a glimpse of your best self. Or, if you're taking good care of yourself now, celebrate that and keep the healthy momentum going. This is a key part of your story. Again, set a timer for five or ten minutes and reflect:

- When in my life did I feel my best?
- Where was I?
- How was I taking care of myself?
- Were my body and mind balanced?
- Who was I with?
- What kind of work was I doing?
- What was I eating?
- How was I moving my body?

Reflect and deconstruct your prime wellness moments. Do you see any patterns that might give you insight into what works best for you? How might you carry this wisdom over into your life now? How can you recreate that level of wellness?

BAJA EPIPHANY

My big "aha" health moment struck while kayaking the Baja (day-dreaming phase). It was a wilderness without mirrors, a land free of societal pressures, and a brief reprieve from my obsession with appearance. The wildlife certainly didn't care what I looked like. Instead of obsessing over my image, I lived in survival mode—moment to moment, focused on taking care of my body so that it could perform at its best. Energy, strength, and health were crucial for the journey.

During that time, I caught a fleeting glimpse of myself in the mirror. Freckles invaded my face, and salt water had matted my braids into dreadlocks that stuck out like Pippi Longstocking. Though I looked like a wild creature that had been lost at sea, I felt as though I'd finally found myself—more comfortable in my own skin than ever before. I had caught a glimpse of a better me; a taste of pure, real, health. Though I initially failed to carry this new perspective with me to the jungle, when I began my studies with IIN, the headspace I'd experienced on the Baja came flooding back.

TALIA POLLOCK, PARTY IN MY PLANTS

Health coach, podcast, and recipes.
Motto: Taking the "hell" out of healthy living.

What was your inspiration to create Party in My Plants?
I created Party in My Plants to breathe fresh, funny air into the often way-too-serious space of healthy living. I've had a passion for comedy, performing, and writing for almost my whole life, and I originally set out in this world to become a professional comedian. But along the way, I stumbled upon healthy eating (specifically, eating plants!), which radically changed my life and helped me overcome nearly a decade of health struggles. Pursuing only one of these two passions—comedy but not healthy eating, or healthy eating but not comedy—felt like cutting off a limb or living in the closet, so I decided to merge the two, and my humorous brand of healthy living, Party in My Plants, was born!

Describe your perfect day.
My perfect day as a Wildpreneur varies greatly, which is a cliché and also in keeping with the "wild" part of the equation. Entrepreneur life is wild, and there's rarely consistency for me, but my favorite days always bookend with meditation and include movement and "me" time first thing in the morning. From there, it's a combination of interviewing guests for my podcast, film-

ing a cooking video, writing my upcoming book, swimming my way out of the email deep-end, having coaching calls with clients or meetings with collaborators, hitting the road for a speaking gig or event, or testing a recipe with friends, an audiobook or a podcast on in the background. And plants. There are always lots of plants being eaten in between things.

Is this your passion? What keeps you motivated?
There's not a chance I'd still be doing this work four years later if I wasn't so deeply passionate about it, because it definitely hasn't been an easy, quick, or tear-free road! What keeps me motivated is both knowing, through gut feeling, waves of success, and literal notes from my audience that this is truly what I'm meant to do with my life—inspire people to take better care of themselves so they can live their best, greatest lives, and knowing that the last thing in the world I want is a "real job." After years of boss-less, bra-less working, I could never not work for myself!

Advice?
The ingredients to my business success smoothie: Pull out what you're uniquely gifted at, combine it with what you're extremely passionate about, sprinkle in a solid reason why you want to do this work as it relates to who you deeply want to help, ignore or outsource that which weighs you down, add some matcha, and blend till creamy. Then drink daily.

What do you wish you'd known?
Just how important the patience piece is to the puzzle. And persistence. I think I would've shed a lot less tears if I had brought as much patience to my business success as I bring to the DMV.

What's your favorite part?
I love making it up as I go! And I love being able to infuse 100 percent of me into 100 percent of what I do so the lines be-

tween "work" and "play" get blurred. Some people might say that it's unhealthy to not have clear boundaries between "work" and "play," but I think blurring the lines has caused me to truly live each day more fully and feel so internally fulfilled than I ever could've imagined, so long as I turn off technology every once in a while.

❋   ❋   ❋

HOLISTIC HABITS

Now that you've considered your past health challenges alongside what has allowed you to be your best self, let's build upon that understanding with some holistic health practices. Note that, although there is no silver bullet solution to health, there are three core concepts that we should mindfully integrate into our Wildpreneur lives daily to maintain balance.

UNO—PRIMARY FOOD

Nourishment begins well before you take a bite. Food is important; it will fill you, but it won't fulfill you, explains Joshua Rosenthal, founder of IIN. Rosenthal encourages us to "Remember a time when you were deeply involved in an exciting project. You believed in what you were doing and felt confident and stimulated. Time seemed to stop. The outside world faded away." Or "Think back to a time when you were passionately in love. Everything was exciting. Colors were vivid. You were floating on air, gazing into your lover's eyes. Your lover's touch and your shared feelings of exhilaration were enough to sustain you."[39] You were high on life.

If you can relate to these sentiments, then you know what it means to feel nourished without food. This has been called "primary food." Love and inspiration are two profound types of primary food. Other sources include exercise, career, relationships, creativity, and spirituality. Take a look at the Circle of Life Exercise[40] below to check in with your primary food. Rate the areas of your life with a dot on the line. The center of the circle is 0 (low score), the perimeter is 10 (high score). When you're finished, connect the dots to see what you are doing well and what needs some attention.♥

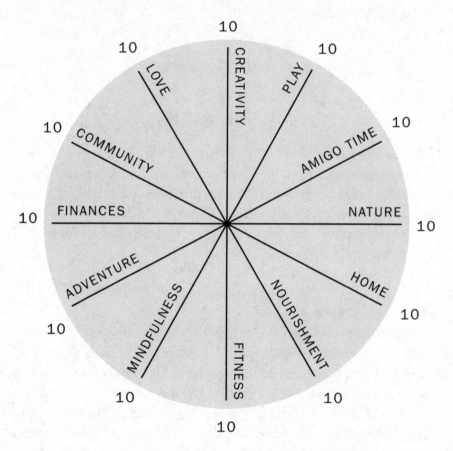

Lifelong Wildpreneur Shannon Hughes says he finds nourishment and balance from "Sunsets, books, music and dancing, even if it's dancing by yourself." For Shannon, watching the sunset every single day is a priority that makes his life as a Wildpreneur possible. "I consider my sunsets very similar to meditation, with a dash of insane beauty. If not for that 45 minutes of beauty-filled silence every day, I doubt I could manage all that I do" says Hughes.

DOS—TUNE IN

Make time daily to listen to your body. What does that mean? Blood is flowing through your veins, your stomach is digesting your food, your brain is creating thoughts. We are walking miracles! But how do we tune in to what's going on inside us? There are some fairly simple ways to tune into your body's intelligence, pinpoint imbalances, and decipher its subtle messages. First, take a break from the culture of speed—slow down, breathe, set aside technology—then use the following tips to go further with tuning in.

TIPS FOR LISTENING TO YOUR BODY ♥

- **Food cravings.** Sugar, salt, creamy, crunchy. May indicate hormonal or mineral imbalances, seasonal change, or dehydration. Your cravings are windows into your body and mind.

  Deconstruct your cravings, understand them. "Cravings will only loosen their grip on us when we commit to stop, listen and learn from them," says cravings expert Alexandra Jamieson. She adds, "When we blindly follow our cravings, without asking what they mean, it's like applying a blunt hammer when what's required is a feather's touch."
- **Whites of your eyes.** Yellowish or bloodshot may indicate imbalance. Look into your own eyes. What do you see?
- **Tongue color.** Pink is healthy, red may indicate inflammation. Stick out your tongue at yourself. What do you see?
- **Skin quality.** Irritation may indicate food sensitivities or hormonal imbalance.
- **Digestion.** Should be smooth, comfortable, and regular. (Don't be afraid to look at your poop.)

- **Energy levels.** Consistently low energy? Something may be out of whack.
- **Mental clarity and mood.** Brain fog might indicate time for a detox.
- **Food sensitivities.** Gluten, dairy, soy, sugar? Take a food allergy test to see what foods might trigger imbalance in your system. A food sensitivity may cause all of the above difficulties.
- **Body types.** There are many tests that will support you in understanding your unique body: Ayurvedic type, metabolic type, blood type, and pH (acid/alkaline balance) are my favorites.

If you find any of these areas to be out of balance, try doing a gentle cleanse (green juices, lots of water, cleansing herbs, cut out dairy, soy, gluten, sugar, caffeine, alcohol, etc.—there are many DIY cleanses). If the imbalance remains, you may consider seeking the support of a health coach or naturopath, either locally where you live or online.

* * *

TRES—NUTRITIONAL FOUNDATION ESSENTIALS

Now let's talk food, finally! Every meal is an opportunity to have a conversation with yourself about which foods will support wellness—today, tomorrow, and in the years to come. Embrace healthy choices and a preventive approach now as you incorporate the following into your daily life:

Dark leafy greens: The most nutritionally rich foods on the planet, and also the food that is most forgotten in modern diets. When you nourish yourself with greens, you will naturally crowd out the foods that make you sick.[41] Green inside = clean inside. Greens support healthy digestion and offer you clean, quality, uplifting energy (plus a plethora of other health benefits). Not a salad lover? There are many delicious ways to eat greens—smoothies, kale chips, soups, and more. Already eating greens? Diversify! Kale is trendy, but there are so many others—spinach, arugula, mustards, seaweed, collards, and so on. There are lots of yummy recipes out there! See Wildpreneurs.com/ health for my favorite quick and simple greens recipe. ♥

Whole food philosophy: Focus your diet on whole foods as nature intended. Don't eat anything your grandmother wouldn't recognize, says food rules expert and author Michael Pollan.[42] Whole eating is a gateway to whole living. Your body appreciates simple, clean fuel such as fruits, veggies, nuts, seeds, beans, whole grains, fish, and sustainable meats (if meat works for you). So many yummy options, you can't go wrong. Do your best to avoid packaged snack foods, this trifecta of processed sugar, salt, and fat is designed to fool your brain so that it loses its ability to discern what it's ingesting (makes it impossible to tune into your body).[43]

Daily TLC: H20, oxygen, sunlight, sleep, movement—these are basic yet essential parts of your nourishment equation.

SHANTI TILLING, SWEATPLAYLIVE

Ten Keys to Wildpreneur Health

1. You are not what you eat, you are what you absorb! If you are eating well but not absorbing all the nutrients, your health (mental, physical, sleep, etc.) can suffer. I highly recommend having a food sensitivity test or doing an elimination diet to really get clear on the proper foods that are right for you.
2. Sleep—Seriously. Get your seven–eight hours. You cannot perform your best as a Wildpreneur or in any aspect of your life if you are chronically tired.
3. Find an exercise you LOVE. Working out should not be a chore. If you do not love your workout, keep searching.

There are so many ways to move your body. Whether it is mountain biking, frisbee golf, CrossFit, barre, or just dancing around your bedroom for a half hour, enjoy it!

4. Make exercise "appointments." Write them in stone in your calendar.

5. Have a Plan B. There are going to be times a kid is sick or your meeting runs late, and you cannot make your workout. Have an exercise video, a regular run, a second exercise class time, or written workout plan that you can do at home. Avoid making excuses.

6. Plan fun into every day. Fun isn't just for weekends. For me, exercise is fun, so I kill two birds with one stone (see #3). My friends and I have Taco Tuesday Fight Night. We box, we eat tacos, and then watch a movie. You may not have four hours to commit to fun, but try to plan at least ten minutes (out of 1,440!) of joy into your day.

7. Get out of your comfort zone. This is a big one for me. I live by Eleanor Roosevelt's quote, "Do one thing every day that scares you." It doesn't have to be jumping out of an airplane. Aerial yoga, or just making an uncomfortable phone call might do the trick. But when you challenge your body or mind physically, you will grow emotionally.

8. Try new things. You are never too old. You may even find a new "favorite thing"! Doing new activities will stimulate neurons in your brain, and that is always a good thing.

9. Breathe in gratitude. I take a few minutes every day to feel grateful. Sometimes it's during my morning meditation or when I walk my dogs. I take deep breaths and thank the universe for x, y, z. It always makes my not-so-good days better and my good days amazing!

10. Breathe some more. I am big on breathing. You can use your breath to calm your mind in the middle of a crazy day (or yoga class), or you can use your breath to

bring power and energy to your body. Long exhalations are scientifically proven to calm your nervous system. I also breathe to power myself up. My close friends make fun of me, because before I do anything "big" like point my bike down a steep trail or speak in public, I always give it a big (loud), quick exhale before I begin.

Bonus: Your Vibe really does attract your tribe! Every single person, animal, and thing on this Earth is energy. We all carry a vibration either positive or negative. All of the above tips are ways to raise your vibration. By eating healthy, getting quality sleep, moving in ways that bring you joy, and stimulating your mind, you are creating positive energy and raising your vibration. In this case, like attracts like and you will attract other people or things vibrating at your level.

* * *

REALISTIC GOALS

Now that your overview is complete, visualize your health in the future. What do you need to work on? How will you invest in yourself and make self-care a priority? Just as you wrote your business plan, create a health plan to guide you along. Return to your Circle of Life Exercise and consider which areas you need to work on. Visualize where you'd like your health to be in six months, and then go backward. Start big (e.g., I want to lose X pounds), then break that down into action steps. There is an art to goal setting, as we did professionally in chapter 4. Try setting yourself SMART goals personally.

As always, don't hesitate to seek support on your journey. Staying on track with health and fitness goals can be tough. Consider working with a health coach or a life coach, join a group support program that resonates with you, or use a friend or fellow Wildpreneur as an accountability buddy.

SACREDNESS IN REVELRY

Siestas and fiestas are also ways to invest in yourself. "Sacredness in revelry," as Jungle Judi says, followed by "and everything in moderation!" Play, eat chocolate, raise your margarita, laugh, these will all nourish your body, mind, and soul. Your health is your most important asset, cherish it. May plugging in your smart phone be a reminder to recharge your personal batteries as well. The health of your bottom line and your personal health are aligned. Return to the notes you made in this chapter again and again. Healthy living as a Wildpreneur starts *now* and continues with every moment thereafter.

DR. KENDALL HASSEMER, ND, NATUROPATHIC DOCTOR

Health, mindset, and yoga educator.
"Always follow your dreams and your heart—even when they seem to drag you through the mud. You might come out a little dirtier, but with a huge smile on your face—for doing what you love and bringing your light and influence into this world."

What are some of the challenges you've encountered as a Wildpreneur?
We are bushwhacking trails for our own journey and the creative spirit that might be a few steps behind us in their own start-up or business endeavors, while simultaneously cruising full-speed-ahead down the highway of curating a physical and social media presence, tackling paperwork and taxes, creating content, and deepening our knowledge of our respective craft. We balance all of these demands while (effortlessly) maintaining mental, emotional, physical, and spiritual well-being.

Yeah, it's wild.

Your favorite part about being a Wildpreneur?

Freedom and playfulness. I feel constrained by the thought of a "normal" workday schedule. Life goes by quickly enough—and to have the flexibility to adjust your schedule is super groovy and an essential part of health, in my eyes. We are wondrous animal beings who thrive on a schedule, but can feel stifled, trapped, and depressed when confined or restricted.

I believe human beings created the present reality of time and a 40+ hour work week. I think the "new-normal," socially accepted construct of a 40+ hour work week is one of the reasons why many people's health is suffering. I want to be part of the movement to step out of our own way and facilitate the return to our health, to our roots—and rewild.

CHAPTER EIGHT

FAMILY BUSINESS: MISSION IMPOSSIBLE POSSIBLE!

HEY, I FOUND YOUR NOSE. IT WAS IN MY BUSINESS.
—ANONYMOUS

"The maid just called in sick," I grumbled. My mom and I sighed as we tugged on our pink rubber gloves and hoisted the buckets of cleaning supplies. We've cleaned many composting toilets together, giggling and whistling our way along . . . or not. There have been gleeful moments, wrathful moments, and every emotion in between. The toilet brush has never been thrown, but working alongside family is no easy task.

"How do you do it?" my guests wonder in awe as they observe my parents and me living, working, and playing together. I've often pondered the same thing. Navigating the challenges of Wildpreneurship as a family has been complex, arduous, and beautiful! Working as a family team is ultimately what has brought the lodge to life and to thrive. It's been a puzzling conundrum; a mission impossible turned inside out.

It's time to put a magnifying glass over the family facet of Wild-preneurship—a must read for any of you adventurers who are considering journeying into business with those you love. In this chapter you'll explore:

- The power of play and finding play that resonates with your family.
- Family fundamentals required for creating a business with those who share your DNA.
- Ground rules for communication, boundaries, and other tips for family harmony.
- What it takes to make a family dream come true.

✳   ✳   ✳

APE AND EXECUTIONER

The first time my mom saw my dad, he was standing naked on the roof of a sauna that he'd built in Alaska. Their paths crossed again five years later at a Halloween party. My mom was disguised as an executioner in a mysterious black mask, and my father sauntered around in an ape costume. When the executioner stepped outside for some fresh Alaskan air and removed her mask, her cascade of blonde hair caught the ape's eye. The sparks flew and their adventures together began. The wind blew them from Alaska to California, Quebec (on the lake where my dad had grown up), Mexico, and beyond. Thirty-five years later, their wild spirits thrive together in the jungle, with a few critical additions—me and my brothers, of course.

Today, the executioner and the ape are known as Jungle Judi and El Tigre, and they've entrusted their daughter as the *jefa* (the boss—

that's me) of our family business. Yup, I write my parents' paychecks—a dynamic that has taken some getting used to. The Tailwind Jungle Lodge has been the ultimate family adventure, however, our journey toward becoming Wildpreneurs together began well before our arrival in the jungle.

A DOLLAR PER MILE

I was a chubby, lazy kid. Ten-year-old me wanted to watch TV and eat candy. My parents had other plans. They were committed to passing on their love of sports and exploration to their kids. I resisted with all my roly-poly might.

"Why would I want to exercise when it makes me miserable?" I moaned. Instead of forcing me, El Tigre chose to entice. My eyes lit up when he waved a five-dollar bill in my face—money clearly sparked my attention. With this in mind, my dad created a system for my brother Rhett and me. Each mile we hiked, ran, biked, swam, kayaked, and so on, would be given a cash value. For example, a mile covered on a bike would be worth 25 cents, a mile run would be worth one dollar, and so on (the value per mile correlated to difficulty). The money we earned went to a special savings account that would fund any kind of sporting or educational equipment that Rhett and I wanted. My mom enthusiastically supported this arrangement.

Suddenly I was *very* motivated. Parents take note—this may be bribery, but it's ingenious! My brother and I meticulously recorded our miles and dollars (this was great for our math skills as well). We proudly earned ourselves our first computer this way. Years later, I recognized that my father would have bought us that computer anyhow. Thank you, clever Tigre, for motivating me!

With this system in place, our family wilderness adventures began in 1993 when my family boarded a train to Nova Scotia. A close family friend, Yves Simard, joined us as we embarked on a 500-mile bike trip self-supported (carrying all our camping gear and supplies) around Cape Breton and Prince Edward Island. Though Rhett and I only carried the sleeping bags and marshmallows, we were empowered by the two-week journey.

As my young muscles adapted to the challenge of pedaling hundreds of miles into brutal headwinds, I discovered that I loved those hard-earned downhills, blissful tailwinds, spectacular vistas, and the thrill of the unknown. As I roasted my marshmallows each night, I began to understand and share my parents' adventurous spirit. It would be the first of many such family expeditions.

THE GLUE—FOUNDATION OF FUN

I must pause our story for a moment here to note that though many factors have enabled us to work and build a family business, I ultimately attribute our success to one key element: PLAY. Frolicking together in the wilderness is a glue that keeps us together. We have intentionally designed our tropical business so that we are never too busy to go surfing or paddling (kayaks, stand-up paddleboards, and any other toy that floats). For us, play as a family isn't frivolous, it's critical for strengthening our relationships, both personally and professionally. Family scholars agree that play can bring families cohesion (bonding time), improve communication, and adaptability. Not only are these qualities invaluable for a family business, our work together has also made us best friends. Though they will always be my mom and dad, we know one another better than a turtle knows its shell.

WHAT IS PLAY?

It's also important to distinguish here: What is play? Play is relative. For us, play = adventure in the wilderness. This may not resonate with your family, but if you're considering going into business together, you must find a form of play that works for your family. What do you all enjoy doing together? Play expert Stuart Brown explains in his TED talk "Play Is More than Just Fun"[44] that there are many different types of play—body play, object play, rough and tumble play, and more. Perhaps for your family, the most beneficial form of play is board games (problem solving) or fishing together (gentle activity). In addition to family bonding benefits, how you play as a family may also be a strong indication of how you work together. Also note that your ability to play together will be critical for lifting spirits when your wild business hits a rocky patch.

MEGAN'S TIPS FOR MOTHERHOOD AND WILDPRENEURSHIP

Freelance writer who created a coworking space, Tahoe Mill Collective

Be efficient. There simply aren't enough hours in the day to procrastinate or linger over a project. It's not going to be perfect and that's OK. Just get it done, move onto the next thing.

The mornings are my time: I leave the kids still sleeping with my husband, and I go out as the sun is rising—for a trail run, to a yoga class, for a swim in the lake. Something to help me start my day with a sense of calm and achievement. If I don't exercise first thing, I often don't get around to it until later in the day. Sometimes, I've stayed up half the night with the baby and I'm exhausted, but I still try to motivate. Having a friend join you definitely helps keep you from choosing to sleep in instead.

You'll be tempted to multitask. Answer emails on your phone while at the playground with your kid. Take a conference call while driving your kid from one thing to the next. Read a work paper at the dinner table. If you can, avoid this. It's nice to just be present and give each aspect of your life—family, work, playtime—the undivided attention it deserves.

Being your own boss sounds glamorous and free. And at times, it is. But other times, it means taking out the trash at the business you started. You'll do everything—big-picture brainstorming and also low-level, nitty-gritty errands. Embrace it all. Try to enjoy the little things.

You won't ever get it all done. There will be a pile of laundry or dishes. A work email left unanswered. A project you just don't have time to complete. And that's OK. You can try again tomorrow.

✳   ✳   ✳

NEW HEIGHTS

Our family playtime took us to high peaks, lakes, rivers, deserts, and beyond as our adventures grew bigger and bolder. Each summer of my teenage years, we headed to Mother Nature's playground. My parents had wisely chosen careers that gave them complete freedom when school was out. My mom worked as a substitute teacher at the local high school while my dad hopped around our neighborhood building custom homes and creative add-ons such as towers, decks, solariums, and saunas. As a master builder/designer (skills he'd acquired from building in Alaska), El Tigre's classic, yet creative, designs grace the shoreline of Lake Memphremagog. His services were always in demand and, though he could have worked throughout the year, he chose his projects and clients carefully. El Tigre's priorities were always clear—family and quality of life trumped extra cash. My parents also rented out our family home each summer (city folk from Montreal love the lake in the heat of July and August), which gave them a bit of extra cash. Their smart and careful budgeting also allowed them to stretch a dollar a long way on our shoestring adventures. Once you own the gear, camping in the wilderness is pretty much free!

As a family, we backpacked California's 220-mile John Muir Trail and Vermont's 270-mile Long Trail, spent weeks kayaking the slot canyons of Lake Powell, ran and surfed the beaches of North Carolina's Outer Banks, and mountaineered Mexico's 18,491-foot Pico de Orizaba. As we reached new heights as a family, each journey fueled our shared passion for play and adventure. These experiences opened our eyes to what we could achieve together, not just as a family but as a team. As I stood atop the summit of the highest peak in Mexico, I peered into the vast crater of the volcano in awe, grateful that my family had pushed me to such a magnificent extreme. What else might we achieve together? The possibilities seemed endless.

A FRESH START

When I headed off to college in Vermont in February 2003, our family was fragmented for the first time, and the distance strained our relationships. Determined to keep our bond strong, El Tigre planned yet another family adventure. In the summer of 2003, we set out on fully loaded bikes from Jackson Hole, Wyoming, and pedaled south nearly 2,000 miles on the Continental Divide Trail to El Paso, Texas. In classic El Tigre style, he'd read about this bike trail in *Outside* magazine years before and had been daydreaming about it ever since.

As we covered miles of dirt roads, the familiarity of adventuring with my family through the wilderness returned. However, that bike trip proved to be our most difficult adventure thus far—trips to the emergency room, violent windstorms, extreme illness, and mechanical issues with our bikes tested our relationships at every turn. Angry shouting matches and tears were frequent and a series of setbacks forced us to hitchhike and adjust our route.

Through the tiresome challenges, my father stayed strong to keep us together, yet revealed a vulnerable side that I'd never seen before. He shared many stories of his life, past mistakes, regrets, and his contentious relationship with his parents. This raw honesty set a new tone for the journey, and we learned to support one another, transcend hardship, forgive, and accept each other's imperfections. No family is perfect. Our relationships grew on a strong foundation of truth, trust, and patience. This new beginning allowed us to cultivate core family fundamentals (described on the next few pages) that equipped us for, eventually, creating the Tailwind Jungle Lodge.

In fact, it was on that Continental Divide bike trip that El Tigre's vision of having a family business began making a regular appearance in our campfire conversations. He envisioned a business that we could create and work on together—a project that would keep us united and preserve our lifestyle of play and adventure, particularly as Rhett and I stepped into life beyond academics. What would that family business be? He didn't yet know exactly. The wheels of my mind began to turn. The following winter (March 2004), we caught our first glimpse of the jungle outside of San Pancho, which is ultimately how I ended up in the Entrepreneur 101 classroom at Middlebury in January 2007, writing a plan for a Jacobi family business.

WHO IS YOUR FAMILY?

Before you move forward, you must also deeply ponder the question: Who is my true family? As you do, keep in mind that there is no "normal family." Every family is unique and unusual. Modern families take many forms. For some, family may not be those who share their blood. Living wild, free, and out of the box may apply to your family situation and dynamic as well. If you feel strong and united with your family (whoever they may be), harness your uniqueness together and channel it into your wild business.

Cayla Marvil speaks of her team at Lamplighter Brewing as family:

I'm constantly motivated by the people around me—from our newest hires to our veteran staff. Each and every person brings an interesting and unique perspective and story to the business; it's amazing to get to know everyone and see them develop and excel in various roles. I want to make them proud!

❋　❋　❋

FAMILY FUNDAMENTALS

Did we have what it takes to build a family business? We wouldn't *really* know until we tried, but journeying through the wilds together had prepared us to hit the ground running into business together. As we reflect on our experience, we see now that we were well equipped with the following family fundamentals:

- **Trust.** If you don't trust one another, you won't get far. Families with a volatile personal mix have buckled under the strain of business.
- **Play.** Find your family bliss regularly. Know how to disconnect from work to reconnect to your personal relationships.
- **Compatibility.** Test your compatibility as coworkers with smaller projects and adventures before diving into something big.
- **Patience.** Your patience will be tested all the time. Can you be patient with one another?
- **Persistence.** Believe in yourself, one another, and your work as a team. Be persistent together.
- **Respect.** It's easy to be casual and neglect professionalism within family business; however, the rules of respect should never be compromised. Be mindful of your tone, words, and attitude toward your coworkers—even if they are siblings or parents.
- **Love.** At the end of the day, you're family. Whatever comes, you *must* stick together. Jaime Acosta, founder of the eco-resort Punta Monterrey, says, "Always remember that no business is worth sacrificing a relationship with a family member."

JAIME ACOSTA,
MONTERREY BEACH RESORT

"There is always something to improve. I think if you reach a point where you think your business is perfect, something is wrong!"

What was your inspiration to get this business going?
Not an inspiration, an ambush! My family asked me to take care of the place. I had just finished my master's degree in environmental engineering. My family wanted to embrace eco-friendly building and sought my advice. I didn't really see it coming. However, I felt committed from the beginning. I knew my family would sell if it didn't work.

Did you make any personal sacrifices to get your business started?
You mean other than completely sacrificing my personal life? Ha! In hospitality, you have a social life, but not a private life. Other challenges have been the summer—intense heat and humidity. But all jobs have ups and downs.

What is the best piece of advice you'd give to a potential Wildpreneur?
Success probably isn't going to come quickly, or cheap, or easily. Don't get desperate, don't be impatient, and be willing to sweat a lot! But know that if you give 100 percent you will get there!

✳   ✳   ✳

CLASH OR JIVE?

Though we were equipped with the family fundamentals, our jungle lodge rigorously tested our family cohesion, forcing us to cultivate new skills. We quickly discovered that family business can bring the joy of building something awesome with the ones you love, which is often accompanied by the difficulty of shared genes that clash instead of jive. We recommend that you take the following ground rules to heart:

FAMILY BRAINSTORM ♥

If you're contemplating creating a wild business with loved ones, expand upon the family fundamentals with these questions:

- What kind of business might I create with my family? What do we do well together?
- Am I ready to spend a lot of time with my family?
- Do we have complementary skills?
- Do we communicate well?
- Are we prepared to be financially involved?
- Can we be patient with one another?

Have each of your family members answer these questions and compare your responses. If your collective answers give you confidence to move forward, then you're ready to give it a shot. Again, you won't really know how you work together as a family until you start, but the answers to these questions should give you some insight.

✱　✱　✱

Clearly defined roles: At the beginning of a family business, everyone is charged with excitement and often more invested than if they were at just "a job." However, as that initial thrill wears off, motivation may waver, and troubles arise when one member of the family isn't giving more than 100 percent. Arguments, disappointments, and disagreements over who is supposed to be doing what can be easily avoided if you clearly outline expectations, roles, responsibilities, and job descriptions. No assumptions—be as specific as possible. This will give your business more structure, professionalism, and help you to avoid squabbles. Defined roles will make everyone more accountable—it will be obvious when someone is slacking off! At your first family business meeting, discuss and have each member answer the following:

- What is my preferred role?
- What will I enjoy most and be willing to commit to?
- What are my strongest qualities, skills, and talents?
- What are my weaknesses?
- What do other members of the family do well? What roles suit them the best?
- What are their weaknesses?
- How can our roles complement each other?
- Who will be the boss?

COMMUNICATION TIPS— THE JUNGLE FAMILY METHOD

"The single biggest problem in communication is the illusion that it has taken place." —William H. Whyte

Decide how you will make decisions as a family team. Though I guide the ship of our ideas, we function as a three-person democracy. Family business meetings are scheduled regularly.

Think and listen before you speak. Pause before responding to conflict. Take a breath, or take all night if you have to (sleep on it!). Watch those "knee jerk" reactions, says Jungle Judi. Quick tempers and thoughtless responses can get you into trouble.

Focus on the big things. It's OK to let little things go (pick your battles), but the big, important things *must* be addressed ASAP—before they can snowball into avalanches!

Strong personalities and reaction styles. Everyone has a different way of thinking and processing, particularly when confronted with conflict and challenge. My mom, the Scorpio, has a fierce sting and is quick to react. El Tigre retreats to the beach to process alone—a reaction I seem to have inherited. Observing and understanding how we each process information has been a conduit for our communication efforts. *How do you respond to challenge or conflict?*

Regular family business meetings. Our jungle rooftop meetings must be in the morning (*before* margaritas!). We take turns speaking and listening and determine how to move forward as a team.

Make criticism constructive and considerate. Criticism between relatives may bite harder than between regular colleagues. Avoid wounding one another with misplaced words by being mindful of the feedback you give family members. Pause before dishing out criticism. When you do choose to speak up, keep it considerate and constructive—it's all in your delivery. Similarly, when receiving criticism, pause before responding and avoid being defensive right away. Keep your ego in check. Focus on opportunities for growth instead of taking things too personally.

Communication is a journey, not a destination. You don't suddenly become masters of communication. It takes work *every single day.* Never give up, it's worth the effort to keep the lines of communication open.

✳   ✳   ✳

Clear communication: Shouting, followed by days of silent treatment, is *not* communication. We've had our share of paltry disagreements—moments when we've called ourselves "The Bickersons." However, we've gradually learned to avoid making mountains out of molehills by improving our communication skills.

Financial divisions: If possible, make finances and compensations as clear and as simple as possible from the start. For some families, a handshake agreement may be enough. For others, written contracts may be necessary. It's crucial to be clear around money. When poorly handled, it can drive a wedge between the members of any family.

Personal understanding: As family, you likely already know one another well. Prepare to take this to a whole new level. If you are open to understanding and supporting each other's emotional patterns, needs, and differences, your work together will flow much more smoothly.

MEN ARE FROM MARS, WOMEN ARE FROM VENUS

The simple understanding that men and women are wired differently can have a profound impact on how you work together and support one another (this is useful for family business and beyond).

As author John Gray explains in *Men Are from Mars, Women Are from Venus*, in day-to-day life, women generally want to feel wanted (women need a listener and empathy), while men generally want to feel needed (they are problem solvers). In response to stress, women are like waves (we crash!), men are like rubber bands (they need to pull away).

Everyone is unique, but acknowledging each other's differences will accelerate your understanding of how best to support each other. As family, your preexisting level of familiarity is an advantage here. For example, my father is "Mr. Fix It" at the lodge. El Tigre does not like to be told what to do, however, he does want to feel needed. With this realization, I've adjusted my approach, wording, and tone. "Dad, could you please help me repair this railing? I would really appreciate your help," goes a lot further than "Dad, you have to fix the railing." See the difference? Though we may be Martians and Venusians, we are learning to speak a common language.

✳   ✳   ✳

Boundaries: The intimacy of family business makes personal boundaries essential. One of the most valuable gifts I've ever received from Jungle Judi is a handmade sign that says "SIESTA." It is accompanied by a rule: When the sign is up, the jungle girl needs personal time. This is a crucial boundary, given that I live in the office.

Establish clear boundaries—personal, family, and business—for both time and space. Some boundaries may be physical (create your sacred space), others are emotional (personal time, no go topics, etc.). In family businesses, "shop talk" can easily spill over onto the dinner table, at birthdays, holidays, and other sacred family moments. If you let business time dominate, you will feel like you're on the job 24/7. Power down and put boundaries in place to keep from burning out and destroying relationships. Don't forget to make family playtime as much of a priority as business meetings! Make play both spontaneous and scheduled.

Unity: Our shared passion for wild living enabled us to create a mission and vision for our business that we all agreed upon—we were on the same page from the outset. Together, we committed to the sacrifices, challenges, and rewards of both the journey and the destination. We're a team, united by a shared dream—a stability that has helped mitigate the many challenges of wild living and ultimately guided us to success. If you're at the beginning of building a family business, establish a core set of values and priorities. "Teamwork makes the dream work!" says John C. Maxwell.[45]

The art of support: Our ability to support each other has made all the difference. We know how to pick each other up, dust each other off, put our heads together to tackle the latest issue, and dive into whatever comes. Though my parents often drive me bananas (they are my parents after all!), they are undeniably what keeps me committed to the business. They taught me the art of support and tough love as they acted as a buoy to keep me afloat through challenges while also pushing me to learn to swim. They empowered me to become stronger and assume the role as leader—*la jefa*. My parents' tireless support has paid off—I'm now able to support and buoy them through difficult times in return.

LABOR OF LOVE

"Would you do it all over again?" a guest asked me recently, as they watched my parents and me guiding a kayaking excursion together. "Absolutely," I responded without pause. It's been a wild ride, but over the years we've managed to turn a three-way tug-of-war into working harmoniously together—most of the time, anyhow! Running a family business is the epitome of a labor of love. We clash and we jive, but at the end of the day, we're eager to wake up and do it all over again. The Tailwind Jungle Lodge is a family dream come true, our ultimate adventure. We're proud to be known as the jungle family—we've become a part of the jungle, and the jungle has become a part of us. Where will our life adventures take us next?

ANELISE AND TYLER SALVO, TAHOE SAILING CHARTERS

Motto: Turning wind into smiles.

SECRETS TO FAMILY BUSINESS

Create a schedule and make it a routine. Taking the thinking out of our days clears up so much headspace to think more about our businesses, our family, and less about who is going to make dinner, who is going to go get the baby when he wakes up, and so on. Create roles for each person and then stick to it. It helps so much and is such a timesaver. Take at least one day off together to go play as a family—no phones, no emails, just people and good times!

Be really clear on what you want out of life. We found that having clear intentions about how you want to live your days informs how you will be living out your years as a family. We knew we needed freedom and flexibility in our daily lives.

Just do your best. At the end of the day, all you can do is try to be as present as possible, work toward your big goals and be a great parent and partner. Some days are completely backward and we both feel like we failed every role we have, and then some days are amazing and we feel like we found a groove. No two days are the same so just accept and move on.

Believe that you can live any life you want. As a family, we have very little fear of living life in a non-traditional way. We know that if we fail, we can always "just get a job," so why not just try running a business together in our wild way?

✳   ✳   ✳

CHAPTER NINE

WHERE'S TARZAN? DATING & RELATIONSHIPS

THE MOST IMPORTANT CAREER CHOICE
YOU'LL MAKE IS WHO YOU MARRY.
—SHERYL SANDBERG[46]

T he free-spirited life of a Wildpreneur is full. Who has time for candlelight, flowers . . . amor? Business drive and romance don't always jive. The human heart is mysterious and complex, but we all crave love from that special someone . . . a Tarzan or Jane to join us in our wildness? But how to find Tarzan or Jane? And once we've found him or her, how to keep that relationship healthy? As with other aspects of Wildpreneurship, embrace the journey of romantic love with an adventurous spirit.

WILDPRENEUR TRAIL MAP #9

In this chapter we will explore:

- Dating, relationships, and marriage as a Wildpreneur.
- Love languages and the kayak test.

- "Couplepreneurship"—when Tarzan and Jane work together to bring a shared dream to life.

✳ ✳ ✳

SEARCHING FOR TARZAN

The legend of Tarzan speaks of his unity with the animals of the jungle. "Because his spirit came from them, he understood them. And learned to be as one with them."[47] Definitely my dream guy . . . sigh. Together we will swing from vine to vine, frolic with jungle creatures, and live happily ever after. The end.

Hah! My voice of reason usurped my romantic heart long ago. My journey of jungle dating has been tumultuous, my Tarzan elusive. In the "get dirty" stage of my business, I barely had time to brush my hair. As mothers do, Jungle Judi worried about my love life. When she recommended I try online dating, I rebutted, "Cyber dating in the jungle is like trying to surf a wave when the ocean is flat." Using technology to find my Tarzan seemed ridiculous. I was happier on my own . . . or was I? The love-sick honeymooners who frequented the lodge and the calls of mating season in the jungle often gave me undeniable pangs of loneliness and envy.

TWITTERPATED

In the spring of 2009, I unexpectedly joined Bambi and the twitterpated. While surfing with some new friends from Colorado, I found waves . . . and romance. He caught my eye and butterflies in my tummy fluttered. Thus began a four-year relationship divided between the jungle and the Colorado Rockies. From powder skiing to surfing, we were in heaven.

Four years later, we came to a crossroads. He had launched his dream business—Powder Factory handcrafted skis—an exciting accomplishment that consumed his days, and my jungle lodge was monopolizing much of my time. As our lives became consumed by our wild businesses, we neglected to make each other a priority. We were also challenged by geographical differences. "Location, location, location," says Cheryl Strayed in her "advice column" podcast, *Dear Sugar*.[48] The question "Where's home?" can make or break a romance. Though our love was strong, that was the end of that. After four years of fun, we agreed to say adios.

JUNGLE DATING

I found myself alone in the jungle once again. Nervous, excited, scared—a confusing emotional cocktail. How to be single? How to date? How to flirt? My answers soon arrived as a septic crisis. The sneaky *tejones* had acquired a taste for sewage, and I was desperately in need of professional assistance. As the septic engineer stepped out of his truck, smelly issues drifted from my mind. I was captivated by Mexican charm, sculpted physique, and gorgeous green eyes. As we talked shit, my flirty giggles echoed off the septic tank.

Then I met his identical twin.

Oh, yes, it was definitely good to be single! Though I didn't end up dating either of these beautiful men, I have strong and lasting friendships with both of them. I also learned the delicacy of dating in a small town and determined that sometimes friendship is a better choice.

Thanks to the twins, my eyes had been opened to dating possibilities, and I was soon wined and dined by a high-fashion photographer in Guadalajara. As I stumbled over my feet at *cumbia* (Latin rock) night clubs and was bewildered by Tapatio and Chilango[49] slang and style, I got a crash course in cultural differences. The jungle girl didn't do so well in the concrete jungle. FYI, to some, *novio* means "serious boyfriend" in Mexico. Oops, I certainly misused that word! Don't make promises you can't keep. After a few weeks, I retreated to the tranquil jungle that I could relate to.

I soon rekindled an old spark with a former guest of the lodge. An ultramarathoner, deep thinker, and generous spirit, he'd chased his dream to become a pararescueman (elite division of the U.S. Air

Force).[50] Though we gave "us" our best shot, we were swimming upstream against the current of our life paths. He took a piece of my heart and gave me country western music. "You and tequila make me crazy, one is one too many, one more is never enough," sang Kenny Chesney on the radio as we said goodbye.

Next, Tinder. Heard of it? I hadn't, until some friends snatched my phone at a wedding, set up my profile, and proceeded to swipe left or right (approving or rejecting potential matches). I awoke the next morning to the ping of a message, accompanied by a photo of a striking guy who conveniently lived just a few kilometers away in San Pancho. Our first surfing date was a surprising success and resulted in him flying me to Bali a few weeks later where he was building a recirculating wave for a water park. Our intense globe-trotting romance eventually smoldered, but I'd certainly learned that online dating can be a good option—many of the couples who stay at my lodge originally met online. However, beware of digital dating fantasies. Social media is far from reality—online flirtation can be a dangerous game.

Though exhausted by the dating game, I gave it another shot when our annual aerial silks (hosted by Disney performer Lauriel Marques de Olivera) returned to the jungle. In class, I swung from the trees alongside a handsome gymnast. Had Tarzan arrived? This guy had certainly mastered the vine swinging thing! Our fleeting weekend romance would turn into nothing but short sweet memories. Flings can be fun but be careful with your heart.

By this point, I'd experienced an array of relationships, from long distance and deep to casual and light-hearted. Across the board, one thing was glaringly clear: I was *not* an easy person to date.

A NEW DIMENSION TO DATING

Wildpreneurs add a whole new dimension to dating—we can be a real challenge to those who dare to get involved! Be mindful of the following as you play the wild dating game:

Last-minute changes. In our wild businesses, challenges arise and plans may be cancelled more often than they are kept. Dates don't like to be stood up. Either make your wild schedule clear, or don't commit unless you know 100 percent that you'll be there.

Interruptions. There is always someone in need of our attention. But we must remember that multitasking may be perceived as rude. Focus on your date. Turn off your phone. Your business will survive for an hour without you. Put someone else on temporary duty.

No days off. Weekends are a foreign concept to us, the lines between work and play tend to blur. But sometimes you've got to turn your work mode completely off and go on an adventure date.

Financial challenge. Your budget may be tight (particularly if you're going the shoestring funding route), but save some pennies for date nights. No need for fine cuisine, but treating your date to tasty tacos and a margarita could definitely pay off.

To-do lists. Don't write your date on your to-do list. This kills romance like a bucket of ice water.

Avoid these classic entrepreneurial tendencies, but don't quit! If you're single, get out there, make time for dating, don't hide behind your wild business. Many interesting people will cross your path.

✳ ✳ ✳

GOODBYE PRINCE CHARMING

By the time I turned thirty-two, I'd kissed my share of frogs. Where was my Tarzan? I was grateful to those adventurous frogs; each of them had taught me much about life, love, and myself. Synchronicity was indeed at play. When your mind is open, you attract like-minded people. You also attract what you need to learn. Perhaps I subconsciously wasn't ready for Tarzan. Or maybe I had the wrong search parameters. So, I made myself a new set of rules:

- **Goodbye Prince Charming.** I needed to design my own happily ever after, to become whole as an individual before finding Tarzan. "Our desire to find one special person who will complete us is hurtful because it is delusional," explains Marianne Williamson in *A Return to Love*. Although popular culture—books, songs, movies, advertising—leads us to feel that we need another person to be complete, I tossed this notion.[51]

- **Timing.** If the timing isn't right, love may not be enough. The cute frogs I encountered may not have metamorphosed into my Tarzan due to circumstances, not heart. You never know when love will show up, but you have to trust that the stars will line up when the time is right.

- **Realistic expectations.** I had been in search of someone to be my everything—my lover, my best friend, my support system, my play buddy. Relationship expert Esther Perel explains that we find one person and "we basically are asking them to give us what once an entire village used to provide. Give me belonging, give me identity, give me continuity, but give me transcendence and mystery and awe all in one. Give me comfort, give me edge. Give me novelty, give me familiarity. Give me predictability, give me surprise."[52] No one person could ever be expected to do and be all that! We must be realistic about what Tarzan or Jane can give.

- **Relationships take work.** In my mind, work was work, romance was all fun, rainbows, and butterflies. Reality check: Real relationships require effort and TLC every single day, just like our wild businesses.

HAPPILY ALONE

In spring 2016, I booked a single room at a ten-day surf and yoga retreat in Nicaragua. I focused on making myself whole with waves and sun salutations (definitely my version of happily ever after!). Post retreat, I closed up my lodge for the summer rains, loaded up my car, drove north through the Chihuahuan Desert with my yellow lab, Paris, as my copilot (she's a terrible navigator but a fantastic listener) and followed my heart back to the Colorado Rockies. As I settled into life in the charming town of Ridgway, nestled in the San Juan Mountains, I felt alive, high on fresh mountain air, and content to adventure solo with my pup. A girlfriend advised me to "Carpe the f**k out of this diem." Paris and I did just that. It was then that pen hit paper, and I began pouring my heart into writing this book.

THE ULTIMATE ADVENTURE OF THE HEART

Then, of course, Tarzan unexpectedly swung into my life—wearing tropical board shorts and a playful grin—in the majestic, snowcapped peaks of Telluride. We began as friends, circumstances changed, the stars lined up, and we've been together ever since. When I wasn't expecting it, I found a fellow free spirit to join me in the wilds. This beautiful man not only speaks the language of the natural world, he's also an adventurer and Wildpreneur. Though it's not always easy, we do our best to flow through life together naturally; inspiring, motivating, and loving each other along the way.

KAYAKING TEST

But how to know when you've found the one that you're meant to share the rest of your life with? Some couples marry after ten years, some marry after a few months, some never marry. As Wildpreneurs, we get to blaze our own trails here, too.

Wondering whether you've found your lifelong Tarzan or Jane? Go for the ultimate test—paddle a double kayak together. This is real-world couples therapy! As Wildpreneurs, we are used to being the captain of our own ships, but with our Tarzan or Jane, we must learn to navigate life together.

I've guided hundreds of couples on kayaking trips in tandem boats (we offer kayaking tours to our guests at the Tailwind Jungle Lodge). I've seen it all and more—couples lost in concentrated silence, couples counting aloud to find their rhythm, couples debating proper technique, couples laughing through the adventure. What kind of couple will you be? Can you work together to make progress or will you paddle in circles? How do you communicate through challenge—are you a "Dead Sea" personality (no talking) or a "Babbling Brook" type (endless chatter)?[53] Some couples ultimately decide that they prefer to paddle their own single kayaks side by side. That's OK, too! Knowing each other's paddling style will give you good insight into your compatibility. Might be a good thing to know before tying the knot.

As you consider paddling through life together, a good question to ask yourself is: "What makes me feel loved and supported?" Or, as relationship expert Gary Chapman asks in *The Five Love Languages*, "What fills your love tank?" He explains that keeping our love tanks full is as important to marriage as maintaining the proper oil level in a car. The challenge here is that Tarzan and Jane may speak different languages of love. While you're paddling, experiment with the following:

Words of Affirmation. Verbal compliments are far better motivators than nagging words. "You're doing great" may be more effective than "Paddle harder." Support and offer words of encouragement. The definition of encourage is to "inspire courage." Help your partner discover his or her untapped potential.

Gifts. Give a shell, a snazzy new life jacket, or the gift of self (don't underestimate the power of presence). Any gift may be an expression of love. My Tarzan calls them "JB" (just because) gifts; no need for a special occasion. "You may always be a saver, but to invest in your loving spouse is to invest in blue-chip stocks," says Chapman.

Acts of Service. Arms tired? Ask your Tarzan (or Jane) nicely if he doesn't mind paddling solo for a bit.

Quality Time. Be present as you paddle together. Listen fully to each other. This can be easy in theory but difficult to implement—practice holding your tongue. Many people don't want advice or even solutions, they just want a sympathetic listener. Don't interrupt, don't give advice unless asked. Simply understand and be there for them.

Physical Touch. When you land at the beach for a break, give your Tarzan or Jane a smooch under a palm tree. For many, touch = love. Tip: Whacking each other with the paddle doesn't count as touch!

It's absolutely worth it to figure out your love language and, of course, your partner's. "Ignoring our partner's love languages is like ignoring the needs of a garden; if we don't weed, water or fertilize, it will die a slow death," says Chapman. Tarzan and Jane must nurture their jungle garden of love.

STILL NOT MARRIED? CULTURAL DIFFERENCES

"Todavia no eres casada?" (You're still not married?) my loyal maid, Claudia, asks me regularly, ever concerned with my love life. She is thirty-five, has three teenagers and a grandchild. "What are you waiting for?" she wonders. I tell her that I'm still searching for my rooster. She giggles and lets me off the hook. My approach to marriage certainly differs from Claudia's. One thing we do agree upon—in Mexico, it's common to be over thirty and living with your parents, I certainly nailed that one!

Cultural norms around marriage and family certainly vary. Go at your own pace. No need to feel pressured or rushed. Blaze your own trail!

✳   ✳   ✳

MARRIAGE AS A WILDPRENEUR

If you've passed the kayak test, is it then time for Tarzan and Jane's tropical wedding? Marriage as an entrepreneur "takes the already complicated institution of marriage to an entirely different level of complexity," says Jay Goltz, small business owner and husband of thirty-eight years. Wildpreneurs' ambition, passion, and free-spirited lifestyle may be both a help and a hindrance to marriage. When you marry, you commit to better or worse. "When you marry an entrepreneur, it might be for *much* better, or it might be for *much* worse. It may very well be both," says Goltz. "How exciting is that? Enjoy the ride. You will never be bored."[54]

Marriage is something I have yet to experience, though it's a journey of the heart I hope to explore at some point. Though I've grappled with what marriage actually means in this modern world (with such high rates of divorce), I do believe in a sacred commitment as life partners and I'm all for a big love fest! Maybe even a white dress . . . I am a romantic after all.

With marriage in mind, I consulted my dear friend, Wildpreneur, and writing coach, Herta Feely, cofounder of Safe Kido Worldwide and creator of Chrysalis Editorial, for some advice. Herta and her husband, Jim Feely, recently celebrated their thirtieth wedding anniversary in San Pancho. An aura of love and respect surrounds the Feelys wherever they go. Herta offered five pearls of marriage wisdom for Wildpreneurs:

1. **Find a partner who is as independent as you are:** While I spend many a weekend writing, my husband golfs and plays tennis. These are very compatible activities, as long as we don't expect each other to do the same thing! Find someone to complement you.

2. **Do the unexpected:** Sometimes I'll send my guy an email love note, and on occasion he sends me flowers for no reason.

3. **Remember to be romantic on occasion:** Find out what your partner considers romantic . . . this may differ between men and women.
4. **Understand your partner:** Definitely familiarize yourself with your partner's love language.
5. **Be flexible:** That's key to everything.

LOVE WILL FIND YOU

If your heart is open and the time is right, love will find you. Tarzan or Jane will show up, so be ready! Keep in mind that Jane can be a little bit crazy and Tarzan can be a little bit silly,[55] and you're all set. When we find the right match and learn to speak the same language, the joy of wild living is oh so sweet. Bring it on, Tarzan and Jane!

PAUL GIRARDI AND DANIELLE HACHEY, COUPLEPRENEURS, FEATHERS AND FUR SURF/YOGA RETREATS

"Do something awesome—chase that which is wild, natural, and free. Just because systems have been set in place in society does not mean we must follow them. Make sure it's awesome for you, for others, and for the environment, and don't stop being awesome!"

Where do you find inspiration as a couple?
The ocean, the trees, and the bedroom ☺.

What was your inspiration to create Feathers & Fur?
Our inspiration for Feathers & Fur was actually founded way back, before we were a couple. I, Paul, was working as a gardener in the small surf town of Ucluelet, British Columbia. I was pruning roses one day down on the inner harbor and Dan-

ielle, whom I had met briefly and was quite taken by, stopped by with a Popsicle. We sat while pruning roses, eating our Popsicles and chatting about life dreams, goals, and ambitions. It turned out we had quite similar desires—to host people and hold a space for people to reconnect to nature, to themselves, and each other. This would have been the summer of 2010.

What challenges have you encountered as couplepreneurs?
Challenges come from every direction, in different shapes, sizes, and forms. The biggest complications we have had seem to have arisen due to something that arguably doesn't even exist—time. Our individual viewpoints on time, and what is pertinent, and when, seem to vary from time to time. Amidst all the "time" we spend together, working, living, and playing, it is in our creation of "what's next" that the "WHEN" really rears its ugly head. But, amidst our busy lives, respecting each other's opinions and reconnecting on our shared goals can overcome petty arguments about when someone did the last Facebook post, or whether we've got up-to-date passports the weekend before leaving for a trip!

Any tips for fellow couplepreneurs?
Remember that your relationship is based on love and togetherness. Not on business. You can argue about marketing strategies, expenses, emails, and whatnot as business partners, but don't forget that those conversations are not what your relationship is based on. Argue as business partners, but then take those hats off and go back to being lovers.

Also, you don't have to do *everything* together. Splitting tasks, and confidently allowing your partner to take it on entirely allows for a bit more freedom. And don't bother trying to share one computer . . .

❋   ❋   ❋

CHAPTER TEN

JUNGLE DRAMA
MEETS ALOHA

THE LONGEST JOURNEY THAT PEOPLE MUST
TAKE IS THE EIGHTEEN INCHES BETWEEN THEIR
HEADS AND THEIR HEARTS. —BILL GEORGE,
LEADERSHIP GURU AND HARVARD PROFESSOR[56]

The jungle allured me with its natural serenity. Yet, I've often found myself flailing in conflict. The mischievous wildlife is no match for anthropological turmoil! I was caught unaware by this complex element of Wildpreneurship. Miscommunications, misperceptions, and disagreements are part of life. How we choose to respond to these inevitable gaps in thinking and philosophy is up to us. Instinctively, we may react with anger, animosity, fear, and even revenge. But might there be a more constructive way forward?

WILDPRENEUR
TRAIL MAP #10 ♥

In this chapter, we will journey through:
- Human drama.
- Using Zen power—thought control, mindfulness, and meditation.

- Riding waves of conflict without drowning in them
- The science of peace and spirit of aloha.
- Practicing communication and conflict resolution with mindfulness, compassion, and professionalism.
- Adding love to the holistic business equation.

✳   ✳   ✳

JUNGLE DRAMA

As in a telenovela (Latin American soap opera), conflict-ridden episodes in the jungle are frequent. We have come to call this "jungle drama." Plots include:

- Mud episode: Torrential rains turn the road into a mud slick. Rental cars and workers' trucks are stuck everywhere.
- Lost yogis episode: A few of our yoga guests drink too much tequila while hiking and take a wrong turn.
- Hot kayak episode: Shortly after purchasing a used kayak in San Pancho, a neighbor confronts us claiming the kayak was stolen from him (we eventually determined that the kayak had actually been swept away with a high tide and drifted ashore in town).
- Suicide episode: An emotionally unstable guest at the lodge threatens to take her life.
- Blackmail episode: A guest surprised that the Tailwind Jungle Lodge is actually in the jungle (?!) threatens to write scathing reviews and call the police.
- Beach access episode: New neighbors block access to a local beach; legal battle ensues.

DEALING WITH CONFLICT

Conflicts grew in complexity, and my agitation compounded. I lived in uneasy suspense at what might happen next. As the years passed, my inner turmoil raged, eventually snowballing into an anxiety attack that knocked me down in the winter of 2016. The attack landed me in the San Pancho hospital in hysterics, my heart jumping in my chest like a hyperactive frog. A compassionate Mexican doctor told me to breathe and try to relax.

Relax? I had forgotten how. Work and busyness had become escape mechanisms to drown out my intensifying inner hurricane. I convinced myself that life would eventually return to "normal." My mind had been an emotional pressure cooker. No wonder I'd exploded! If you're waiting for "normalcy" to return, you may spend your life waiting. What is normal for Wildpreneurs? There is no such thing.

As I pondered where I went wrong, I flipped through my journal and landed on this entry from 2009. "Once I get a grasp on my physical health issues, my mind and emotional wellness will have some catching up to do." No kidding—my prediction had certainly come to fruition. Don't neglect your psychological health. I hadn't cultivated the emotional tools needed to work through the torrent of conflict. My holistic nutrition studies with IIN had taught me that the mind and body are inextricably intertwined, but it had taken an anxiety attack for me to *finally* register that truth. Wildpreneurs must make friends with our minds, but how?

WELCOME TO THE WOO WOO CLUB

"Jungle meditation tomorrow at 7 a.m.," announced the radiant yoga retreat leader. I cringed as I recalled my initial attempt at meditation during one of the first retreats we hosted at the lodge. An hour of sitting in silence with my legs crossed had felt like an eternity of torture. Following that experience, I'd declined countless invitations to meditation sessions and resisted joining what I'd labeled the "woo

woo club" as they chanted mantras and decorated themselves with shells and feathers.

Now the tide had turned, and I was envious of those seemingly unencumbered yogis. I wanted whatever Zen cocktail they were having. A real cocktail was also tempting. Margaritaville offered tasty relief at every turn—a quick way to dull my emotional distress. Yet, I knew enough to see that a margarita (or two or three) would ultimately worsen my emotional problems. As global spiritual leader Thích Nhất Hanh[57] explains: "When our minds are full we often have the urge to fill, distract or numb with junk food, junk entertainment, anything to keep our minds off our troubles. We may succeed in numbing for a little while, but the suffering inside wants our attention and it will fester and churn until it gets it." If I pushed my emotions aside, they would undoubtedly find a way to rise up, and I had no desire to return to the hospital anytime soon.

Thus, my new desperation to heal my psychological calamity drove me into meditation class once again. As I sat apprehensively on my yoga mat, the yoga teacher began. "We will start with a three-minute mindfulness session lying down, then do some stress-relieving breathing exercises." I raised my eyebrows in surprise. *Really? Laying down sounds very appealing . . .*

WHAT IS MEDITATION?

Fifteen minutes later, I lay transformed. The meditation had been a soothing aloe to my psychological wounds. I felt an overwhelming sense of strength and ability to handle whatever the world might throw at me. Flummoxed, I wondered, what exactly is meditation?

Meditation is described as the process of clearing your mind. It is an invitation to observe what is going on with our thoughts and emotions, and then to let them go. When a thought arises, rather than squelching or obsessing over it, American Buddhist Pema Chödrön recommends acknowledging it, "without calling it names, without hurling rocks, without averting your eyes."[58]

BARKING
DOGS

"In Nepal the dogs bark all night long. Every twenty minutes or so, they all stop at once, and there is an experience of immense relief and stillness. Then they all start barking again. . . . When we first start meditation, it's as if the dogs never stop barking at all. After a while, there are those gaps. Discursive thoughts are rather like wild dogs that need taming. Rather than beating them or throwing stones, we tame them with compassion. Over and over we regard them with the precision and kindness that allow them to gradually calm down. Sometimes it feels like there's much more space, with just a few yips and yaps here and there."
—Pema Chödrön, *When Things Fall Apart*

✳ ✳ ✳

In addition to soothing the barking dogs, meditation has been called "the miracle drug." Arianna Huffington explains there is nothing simpler, yet so powerful as meditation. It makes her feel organized and happy and able to face the challenges of the world.[59] She offers countless studies that show that meditation and mindfulness training benefit every aspect of our lives—our bodies, minds, physical health, and our emotional and spiritual well-being. Meditation may actually switch on the good genes (the ones that boost immune system, reduce inflammation, etc.) and can physically change our brains (the thickness of the prefrontal cortex).

That all sounds pretty good, right?!

WHEN THINGS FALL APART

Craving further guidance, I quickly learned that I needed to stop fleeing and start being. Chödrön invites us to practice "relaxing amidst the chaos, learning not to panic." As I digested this, I wondered: How can Wildpreneurs gracefully ride waves of conflict instead of drowning in them?

POOR INTERNAL COMMUNICATION

With that, I took a baby step forward and committed to observing my mind. As I tuned into my thoughts, I was alarmed by the perpetual high-speed chatter that bounced from one issue to the next as I relived the past and worried about the future. My internal communication was like a staticky radio that jumped from one channel to the next.

With this realization, meditation and mindfulness became key components of my Wildpreneur toolbox. Adding a few moments of mindful breathing or meditation to your daily routine costs nothing, but offers much. No promises, no guarantees, this isn't a silver bullet solution, but given the wildness of our journey, finding an inner calm will give you a reliable reprieve from the storm. I urge you to give it a try.

MEDITATION AND MINDFULNESS

Mindfulness is my preferred form of meditation, but note that there is a difference between the two. One of my favorite yoga teachers, Yael Flusberg, elaborates:

Meditation: There are many forms of meditation. Traditional meditation is sitting still so you can learn the patterns of the mind. May also include visualization exercises.

Mindfulness: Mindfulness is a form of meditation. It may be a state of stillness or flow so long as you apply your complete attention to either object or a practice, which is "mindful action." Mindful action may be applied to whatever you like—gardening, trail running, swimming, even mindful dishwashing.

GET STARTED

There is a reason why meditation and mindfulness practices have become popular. There are many ways to get started; find the meditation/mindful practice that works best for you. I recommend starting out with short meditations that are effective and easy to integrate throughout the day. Even a few minutes of mindfulness can make a difference. Simply inhale and exhale deeply, reconnect your mind with your body as you breathe. If possible, close your eyes, try putting one hand on your heart and one hand on your belly to reconnect body and mind.

If you have difficulty doing this alone, consider guided meditations. Check out classes in your local community center, yoga studio, stream-guided meditations online, or try a meditation app.

MEDITATION MYTHS ♥

Sit like an awkward pretzel. Traditionally, meditation can be practiced in four positions: sitting, standing, walking, and lying down. I believe that there is no right or wrong way. It's *all* good! I often practice mindfulness in motion: running, swimming, and road biking. Find your style.

Meditation takes years to learn. You don't need to practice lengthy meditations to enjoy the benefits. Furthermore, if you start moderately you'll be more likely to stick with it. Don't expect to be a master right away. "You don't learn to sail in stormy seas," says Buddhist monk Matthieu Ricard (known as the happiest man in the world). It takes practice.

Think of nothing. Meditation is about greeting thoughts with kindness, compassion, and respect. As portrayed in the clever animated film *Inside Out*, even the character of sadness must be allowed to express itself. However, as the director of our own lives, meditation gives us the opportunity to acknowledge all emotional characters and decide which will play the leading roles.

I'm too busy. Even a 60-second mindfulness pause works. Consistency is what matters. You're never too busy to spare a minute.

Meditation is only for times of stress. Meditation is a practice of cultivating mental tools to deal with challenges. Prepare yourself for stressful times by practicing regularly.

Post-meditation enlightenment. Don't assume that you'll end up blissed out after meditation. Sometimes you'll be full of frustration, anxiety, and relentless thoughts. That's a sign that healing is underway! Let those emotions rise and be released, like bubbles in seltzer.

✷　　✷　　✷

Meditation too woo woo for you? Call it whatever you like. I now use the term "mindfulness pauses." Big wave surfer Laird Hamilton has his own version as well. He says to "breathe until you see yourself." In his class, he guided us through deep belly breathing at a fast, intense pace, followed by holding our breath for a long period to calm the stress response. The resulting physical and psychological sensation is intense and beautiful: tingles, buzzing, mental clarity, calm . . . bliss. When Laird is taken out by a big wave, his breathing techniques make all the difference to his survival.[60] Mindfulness and meditation practices may be key to our survival as Wildpreneurs as well.

MANDY BURSTEIN, ZEN GIRL CHRONICLES AND MODERN HEALER YOGA

Motto: Create a fire in your heart, transform your life, and activate the greatest healer you'll ever know: YOU.

The ebb and flow of energy, especially in a business setting is a fascinating thing to witness. The Universe mirrors your energy. The times when I'm most successful at launching an event, collaborating on a project, or something as seemingly small as teaching a one-hour yoga class, is when I put my whole heart into it. Everyone involved can feel your passion, and it ripples out into a beautiful flow of support and success from there.

Any wild wisdom to share?
I believe that the old paradigm of working for someone else your whole life is crumbling. The more empowered we become, the more we are realizing that each choice we make in life is important. And the choice of where, how, and who you work for is one of the biggest you'll ever make! Know that the path of the "Wildpreneur" is not an easy one. But it will be the biggest opportunity for spiritual growth, and the key to unlocking your freedom.

✳   ✳   ✳

THOUGHT CONTROL = ZEN POWER

I gradually strengthened my mental muscle as I practiced mindfulness moments on the yoga mat, in the waves, in line at the grocery store, in traffic. The following became clear:

- **We control our mind, it doesn't control us.** It's up to us to take the reins and show our mind who is in charge.
- **Evict the negative.** We all have the ability to let go of much negative thought chatter. With a glass half-full mentality, we may prevent small issues from becoming magnified into major crises. Though some negativity is part of being human, we can distinguish between constructive anguish and useless rumination.[61] You get to control *who* crosses the

threshold of your mind. Sometimes, "You have to kick people out of your head as forcefully as you'd kick someone out of your house if you don't want them to be there," says Amoruso. "Focus on the positive things in your life and you'll be shocked at how many more positive things start happening."

TIPS FOR LETTING GO OF THE NEGATIVE

Rewire. There is always something positive to refocus your attention on.

Find a physical outlet for negativity. Go walking, try yoga or boxing. Let the negativity come up, evaporate, and be replaced with happy endorphins.

Daily gratitude breeds positivity. At the end of the day, list three things you are grateful for.

Surround yourself with mindfulness mantras. The walls of my casita are decorated with signs like "one day at a time" and "life is a beautiful ride." Reminders help!

SIMPLE MEDITATION FOR WILDPRENEURS

Mantra: Release tension, set intention.

Close your eyes for a minute (or two or three). On the exhale, repeat the mantra "release tension" in your mind. As you do, feel your body relax. As you inhale, set a fresh intention. What positive steps do you want to take next as you move through your day? Replace any sensation of depletion with healing energy.

* * *

- **Intuition.** When we calm the chatter of our minds, we create space for our inner wisdom to guide us. "If we learn to listen, intuition is like a tuning fork that keeps us in harmony" says Huffington.
- **No mud, no lotus.** As we learned on the Baja (daydreaming stage), any situation is an opportunity for growth. Thích Nhất Hạnh tells us, "If you know how to make good use of the mud, you can grow beautiful lotus." When we examine what we really want, we realize that everything that happens in our lives—every misfortune, slight, loss, joy, surprise, and happy accident—is a teacher, and life is a giant classroom. What we choose to do with each lesson, how we assimilate it, is up to us. Arianna Huffington also believes that "There is a hidden purpose—and alchemy—in suffering that's transmuted into wisdom and strength."
- **Presence.** We can *always* come back to the present.

By incorporating these thought control discoveries, I felt as though I had a Zen superpower. I began to perceive life as a series of moments, like pearls strung together in a necklace of opportunity. I felt awakened to the deliciousness of the now. On March 8, 2016, I wrote in my journal:

BEING PRESENT IS NATURAL. WHY WOULDN'T YOU WANT TO BE PRESENT? EACH MOMENT IS A FRESH START. LET GO. LOVE. Making friends with my mind had simultaneously opened my heart.

SARAH LOVE, I STAND FOR LOVE

Calendars and gifts that uplift and inspire.
Motto: Your love changes the world.

What was your inspiration to create I Stand For Love?
Years ago, I literally woke up in the middle of the night with those four words in my head. It sounded so simple yet powerful and I thought if people said these words the world would change. I had an inspirational art business going, but I wanted it to be more universal. More about the power of love than about me as an artist. So, I changed everything to I Stand For Love and even created an international holiday on August 8 called I Stand For Love Day.

My deepest desire is for future generations to feel more love in their own hearts and I think this is a crucial time for us to make a shift in that direction. I believe in the power of the collective and the more of us that turn toward love, the more we will increase that vibration in the world. My mission with I Stand For Love is to be a little wave of positivity and hope to uplift human hearts every day.

Is this work your passion? What keeps you motivated?
Yes! It really has to be a passion or it would be hard to stay self-motivated for me. What keeps me motivated are other individuals who are using their energy to create a ripple of change. Big or small, I love hearing about people doing awesome things. I truly believe that we are living in transformational times. This is not the hour to stick my head in the sand, this is the time to bring my heart fully into life.

How do you give back to your community?
Giving in general is an important piece of my business model. I donate my inspirational calendars to a few nonprofits every year. Last year I upped my game and was able to donate 400 calendars to the volunteers and the Crisis Text Line and 450 to the Immigrant and Refugee Community here in Portland, OR. I love to give the daily inspiration to people that might not have access to art or messages of hope like that. I also have free art nights in my studio for friends. I donate money to a handful

of environmental organizations too and do lots of research before I make any products. I have a no plastic policy with my product line and print everything locally. There's always more I want to do for people and the Earth. It never stops being a priority for me.

* * *

WILDPRENEURSHIP WITH LOVE

Empowered and excited by my progress, I posted a heart-shaped sticky note on my bathroom mirror. I resolved that love would be the ultimate antidote to jungle drama. "You just have to make your decisions out of love. And when we make decisions out of fear, that's when we have problems" says Arianna Huffington.

The word "love" is used to express many different things, but I think we can agree that "I love tacos" does not carry the same weight as "I love you." The flavor of love I posted on my mirror is the kind of love that you carry with you at all times. It's a caring, compassionate, nonjudgmental energy that you project to strangers and friends alike, a light that radiates through the darkness; the energetic signature that you leave everywhere you go. This type of love is our road to resolution and peace.

THERESA ROTH,
SUPERLOVETEES

"I am constantly motivated to spread love, and good vibrations everywhere, and lucky enough to have an outlet for that."

What was your inspiration to create SuperLoveTees?
It was an "accident." I had a line of cashmere panties I was making and selling on Etsy, and decided to make some T-shirts

during the warmer seasons. It took off, and I never went back to the first idea.

What advice would you give to a potential Wildpreneur?
1. Start where you are
2. Use what you already have

What do you wish you'd known prior to getting started?
You don't have to be perfect or have a perfect product to start.

What's your favorite part about being a Wildpreneur?
That I can't really make a mistake. When working in the corporate world, I had a lot of anxiety about making mistakes. Now, I can try things and if they don't work, it's just a learning experience.

✻   ✻   ✻

PEACE + LOVE = HOLISTIC BUSINESS♥

Now that we're equipped with mindfulness and loving intention, how can we translate these into practical tools for conflict resolution and working through challenge? Wildpreneur Walter Wright, creator of *SAILWIND,* educational adventures and science-based conservation, believes that though there is no exact methodology, there is an art to communication and conflict resolution with mindfulness, compassion, and professionalism.

Wright's approach merges two concepts: *paciencia* (Spanish and Portuguese word for patience, derived from "the science of peace") and the spirit of Aloha. He explains that, in Hawai'i, to live Aloha is to live in unity and harmony with yourself and all life forms around you.[62] Aloha is a code of conduct, an attitude, and a way of life fueled by love. Add the science of peace to this, and you've got a powerful combo.

Wright and I collaborated to offer you the following guidelines for thoughtful communication as a Wildpreneur:

- **Be respectful.** To others, yourself, and your business. Even if on different pages, treat others how you want to be treated.
- **Set intention.** Approach challenges with an outcome beneficial to all. "Go into situations with what you want to find there," says Huffington.
- **Communication.** Be very clear with your wants and needs. Be mindful of your tone and phrasing. Take turns speaking, make sure the other is finished before you speak. Breathe before responding. Ask clear and straightforward questions.
- **Beware of miscommunications.** The majority of conflict arises from lack of information, poor information, no information, or misinformation. With the short replies of texts and emails, miscommunications are happening more frequently. Figure out the best method of communication: phone, face to face, email, and so on.
- **Be humble.** Stay open to other viewpoints. "Without the baggage of what we think we know, we make room for ourselves to grow," says Laurence G. Boldt, author of *Zen and the Art of Making a Living*.
- **Mutual benefit.** Seek common ground. The best way to avoid conflict is to help those around you achieve their objectives. Hidden within most conflicts is a seed of opportunity.
- **Hear it.** Be an active listener—echo their thoughts back to them in your own words to confirm that you understand. Ask for clarification if necessary.
- **Personal understanding.** It's not always about agreeing. A great goal is to look at the other person not with blame or criticism, but rather with understanding and compassion. Step into their shoes, empathize with their perspective if possible. You can disagree and still have a good relationship. There is no right or wrong.
- **Prevention.** Be proactive when possible. Many conflicts can be avoided or minimized by identifying potential issues and speaking up before the situation escalates.

- **Be firm**. Not stubborn, there is a difference; stubborn doesn't allow for compromise.

- **Sleep on it**. Take a mindfulness pause, breathe or sleep on it before responding. Knee-jerk reactions are typically driven by emotions. Say nothing instead of reacting in an inflammatory way. "I can't respond to this right now" is an acceptable response. Let emotions cool so you can both think more clearly. Paciencia is key here.

- **Forgiveness**. When confronted with deep conflict, we must ultimately forgive others and ourselves. When we forgive, we're clearing something from our mind and giving both sides permission to move on. We are freeing ourselves from taxing emotional baggage. Forgiveness doesn't mean naivety. Learn along the way (tune into the lessons!) but let go of toxic animosity. "Forgiveness is not a feeling; it's a commitment. It is a choice to show mercy, not to hold onto the offense against the offender. Forgiveness is an expression of love," says Gary Chapman.

BETTER, NOT BITTER

Though wild living will bring its twists and turns, we mustn't succumb to conflict and drama. We may ride some crazy emotional waves and flounder a bit, but we will catch our breath. Instead of getting bitter, we get better. Find your Zen, focus on silver linings, and let the lotus blossom. Jungle Judi has found her Zen, she says, "To face the challenges, I have adopted the attitude that it is very important to keep karma good. We are human, we have egos, but we need to draw on our spirituality and love, even when you feel someone deserves to be yelled at, hah!"

As jungle drama continues to present itself in unexpected ways—we breathe, pause, assess, summon *paciencia,* and call upon the spirit of Aloha to work through conflict as lovingly as possible. When jungle mud strikes, we do our rain dance, marvel at heart-shaped leaves,

teach our guests the Spanish word for "slippery," and prepare for the adventure of pulling our neighbors out of the ditch with our 4x4 Jeep Wrangler. No mud, no lotus, right?

TOTO FLORES, MEXICOLATE (ARTISANAL CHOCOLATE)

Our mission goes to the heart of humanity and awakens goodness, truth, and love.

What advice would you give to a potential Wildpreneur?
Do things from the heart. If what you do generates a positive change in others, the universe makes the engine work.

What do you wish you'd known prior to getting started?
Trust the flow of it all, that everything will work out as it should. A mysterious force guided me to become involved with the cacao and its energy, it really is magic! I've learned that everything is perfect with all its imperfections. Our working model is somewhat unconventional, but our system works naturally. Our team works well together, strengths and weaknesses complement each other.

What keeps you motivated?
Sharing with people all the magic that cocoa gives us keeps me motivated; the love and joy people bring and share when they're in our little chocolate shop. Then they recommend Mexicolate to more people who bring their love and joy to the shop. It's just this beautiful cycle. That gives me motivation to bring abundance and joy to many hearts.

What's your favorite part about being a Wildpreneur?
Living outside the box. I make it a priority to connect with customers as friends and fellow humans. I love to open hearts.

How do you give back to the community of San Pancho?
I am so grateful to this place, the people, the nature that surrounds us. We are planting cocoa trees for the downtown to
have more cocoa in the future. We offer cocoa workshops to
children and try to give chocolates or cocoa water at community events and we make it a priority to hire local people to
support the economy of San Pancho. I also personally volunteer with many sustainable efforts in town.

✳   ✳   ✳

UNITY

The world always needs more love. Wildpreneurs blaze a trail of
peace, connection, compassion, empathy, and love. It is critical that
we connect with our innermost essence—do the work on ourselves to
find serenity within our emotional worlds—so that we may navigate
life and business with an open heart and guide others to do the same.
Not everyone will love you back, and that's OK. We must not let
anyone walk with their dirty feet on our minds.[64] As we confront the
challenges of life, we must raise ours words, not our voices. It is rain
that grows flowers, not thunder.[65]

Humans are complex emotional creatures, but in the end, we all
need love. There is nothing more important.

SOFTEN THE WALLS OF YOUR WILD HEART

Kelly Guenther, a yoga teacher at the lodge, offers us the Metta prayer
for times of conflict. She explains that this meditation increases our
ability to be more compassionate and loving toward ourselves and
others. It takes away the constriction on your heart, the person, and
the situation.

Part 1: Sit quietly. Close your eyes. Rub your hands together and
place them on your heart.

Repeat aloud several rounds in full voice gradually getting quieter.

May I be healthy
May I be happy
May I ride the waves of my life
May I live in peace no matter what I am given[79]

Part 2: Now envision whoever you are having a conflict with. Repeat with palms open at your sides and replace the word "I" with "you"

Part 3: Finally, envision the entire world and repeat, replacing the word "I" with "we"

SUSAN HORNING AND NICOLA BENNETT, UNITY YOGA TEAHOUSE

Yoga, tea, and good company in Vancouver, Canada.

Your favorite part of life as a Wildpreneur?
Sue: My favorite part is the "FREEDOM!!!" to make choices that are in line with my fundamental values and to vote with every dollar I make and spend.

Any advice?
Nicola: Look for like-minded individuals to collaborate with and everything will run smoother. The people really make all the difference in your experience so make sure you pick them wisely!

Personal sacrifices you made to get your business going?
Sue: Sacrifice and discipline are two things that I feel are required for businesses to be created and sustained, but to enjoy the process should always be our priority! By evaluating each decision as it arises and not making generalizations or

too many rules, I feel more capable of navigating challenges and opportunities, and remain flexible enough to move forward with my endeavors.

Anything else to share?
Sue: I really feel that the foundation of being a Wildpreneur is ultimately creative and that we are all here to express our highest truth through freedom. By focusing on what comes naturally, following the path of least resistance, and fostering relationships based on truth, patience, loyalty, love and trust, the way forward becomes intuitive, logical, and very rewarding.

✳   ✳   ✳

CHAPTER ELEVEN

CHASING INSPIRATION

LIFE IS NOT MEASURED BY THE NUMBER OF BREATHS WE
TAKE BUT BY THE MOMENTS THAT TAKE OUR BREATH AWAY.
—VICKI CORONA, PROFESSIONAL DANCER[66]

WILDPRENEUR TRAIL MAP #11 ♥

How do we keep our inspiration flowing? In this grand finale chapter we discover:

- The art of keeping inspiration alive.
- Core principles to guide Wildpreneurs on their journey.

✳   ✳   ✳

A DECADE

"Surprise!" they greeted me. My eyes lit up at the sight of my closest jungle amigos standing on my rooftop grinning at me. I laughed as they perched a sparkly, pink, fish-shaped hat on my head and handed me a margarita.

"What are we celebrating?" I asked, confused. "It's not my birthday . . ."

"Our ten-year anniversary, silly," my mom responded happily, looking radiant in a dress decorated with tropical blossoms.

El Tigre winked at me from under his Panama hat and hoisted his glass. "Cheers to a decade of jungle living," he announced.

Everyone raised their glasses. "To the jungle family!" they cheered.

"To the jungle!" I responded joyfully.

My friends launched into animated tales of their experiences with the jungle family and the lodge—inspiring moments, "oh shit" moments, aha moments, and everything in between. I sipped my margarita (sacredness in revelry) and listened contemplatively, savoring the magic of the moment. I felt alive with gratitude, happiness, peacefulness, excitement, and awe at what we'd created. Ten years of wild living and the jungle—it still takes our breath away, just as it did that first day we sprinkled tequila to break ground. I wouldn't change a single thing, I think to myself. Hah! Well, maybe a couple. But the speed bumps sure have taught us some valuable life lessons.

Cheers to you, too, fellow Wildpreneur. We have much to celebrate. Life is good!

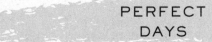

PERFECT DAYS

Mike Rosenburg—Garuka Bars

There is nothing more fulfilling than seeing a passionate idea of yours turn into a successful reality. Except maybe doing all that, and going skiing for a few hours during the day, too!

Nico Blevins—Acupuncturist

The only common denominator in a perfect day as a Wildpreneur for me is the peace of mind/body/spirit that comes from the realization that I am free—that I am not bound by fear or conventional thinking. That my success is limited only by myself, and that the more vibrant in life and health I can become, the more successful I will be. Mix all of that in with living in a tropical paradise and most days could be defined as "perfect."

Shanti Tilling—SweatPlayLive
I LOVE getting to create my days. I love exercising, I love teaching, I love personal training, and I get to do what I LOVE every day!

✱　　✱　　✱

CODE OF LIVING FOR WILDPRENEURS

Now that we've explored the essence of Wildpreneurship, the next question is, how do we keep our inspiration flowing? Through writing this book, I've discovered that there is an art to chasing inspiration. Though we may embark on the journey of Wildpreneurship from different places—for some it's passion and daydreams, for others it may be DNA or synchronicity—once we're on the trail, common forces are at play. There is a pattern to the stories of the Wildpreneurs that I interviewed for this book and whom I've met along the way.

We are all works in progress, always striving to improve—our work, ourselves, and beyond—in our own unique ways, at our own pace. We don't perceive life as a race to the top, in fact, Wildpreneurs will never reach the summit of our adventures because our visions continue to grow grander and higher—fueled by inspiration, love, and appreciation of life. The beauty is in our journey—the people, the places, the lessons, and experiences—not only the destination. We believe in the power of one but strive to grow together. To keep the journey flowing, we must continue our quest for inspiration. The following principles may help us on our way as holistic Wildpreneurs:

PRINCIPLE #1—AWESOMENESS FACTOR

As Wildpreneurs, we're constantly making decisions—choosing our path as we encounter many forks in the road. Fellow Wildpreneur Paul Girardi (surfing teacher and retreat leader) offers us a playful, yet practical guideline for daily decision-making called "The Awesomeness Factor" that will support us with keeping inspiration alive.

Paul describes this theory as "chasing that which is wild, natural, and free. Just because systems have been set in place in society does not mean we must follow them." He explains that when you make a decision, make sure it's awesome for you, for others, and for the environment. Paul claims that this "complex theory" was derived through countless years of study, a philosophy degree, and spontaneous living. Read carefully:

1. You have a scenario you are torn about. Possibly a decision to be made or something causing you turmoil.
2. Lay out your options, keeping in mind the awesomeness factor. Open your mind to explore the various possibilities with your dilemma/scenario: possible outcomes, options, directions you could go.
3. This is the big one: You pick the MOST AWESOME option and do that one. You commit to it. You stick to it. You keep following that awesomeness. And never

stop. Keep picking the awesome option, and you will never fail.

"That, in a nutshell, is the awesomeness factor," says Paul. "It's living life knowing you've made the decisions you have for a reason based solely on awesomeness and positivity—not fear, or expectations, or judgment. And that, is going to be an awesome life."

Gracias for this wisdom, Paul! As we come to forks in the professional road of life, may we be guided by awesomeness, while also being awed at the world around us and ourselves: We are walking miracles. "In every outthrust headland, in every curving beach, in every grain of sand, there is a story of the earth," says Lewis Blackwell in *The Life & Love of the Sea*. If our awe and awesomeness ever begin to falter, may we reignite our inspiration by practicing *vuja de*,[67] seeing something familiar with fresh eyes (the opposite of déjà vu). Do this and the word "boring" will never be part of our vocabulary. The inspiration is sure to flow.

PRINCIPLE #2—REDEFINING SUCCESS

Living by our own definition of success is another catalyst for keeping the inspiration flowing. Success has been traditionally based around the pursuit of two metrics: power and money. "The mad drive for these two conventional goals can be unhealthy to the point of being fatal," says Arianna Huffington.[68] We Wildpreneurs are driving a paradigm shift: success isn't some elusive destination or goal down the road, success is now. We opt out of the old game "Simon Says"—no thank you, status quo. We refuse to live on auto-pilot or define life by GDP. Instead we focus on GWB—general well-being (something that can't be measured with money). For us, success means blazing our own unique trails through beautiful landscapes, cultures, and relationships. It means designing our lives and our work intentionally with a focus on quality of life every single day. We define richness as abundant time, freedom, inspiration, and just enough money to make our lifestyles work comfortably.

If life is here and now—let's live it up! We are free-spirited rene-
gades, courageous enough to step out of the box to follow our daydreams and our hearts. With this new definition of success, we also
have a supportive tailwind at our backs—when things get hard, those
who are just chasing dollars may not have the fortitude to stick with
it, whereas we Wildpreneurs are driven by the strength and commitment that come from following our purpose, passion, and inspiration.
We have innate perseverance and grit! Fellow Wildpreneurs propel
our new definition of success:

*It's not easy to do in today's world, but we must remind our-
selves that we have the power to choose where and how we
spend our energy, and that when we persistently align ourselves
with our deepest callings and desires, we can attract what is
needed to do what we really want to do. When we live from
heart-space, there is always a way. Turning away from the "se-
curity" of a job we don't love or a situation that no longer suits
us is a scary leap, but there is so much to gain when we prioritize
our personal values and happiness.*

—CAPTAIN LIZ CLARK[69]

*I prefer to see my life as a tree, branching out in who knows
what directions. There is never a destination, just the impulse to
grow. My only policy throughout has been to keep an open mind
and, whatever I do, to give it my all. It still takes my breath away
to think where that simple outlook on life has taken me, how
many times I have managed to defy what I thought possible.*

—CHRISSIE WELLINGTON,
IRONMAN WORLD CHAMPION AND
AUTHOR OF *A LIFE WITHOUT LIMITS*[70]

PRINCIPLE #3—HARD WORK

Chasing inspiration takes work; we have to earn it. First, we choose our work wisely—go deep within to attune to the things that we know we were put on this planet to do. Then, once we've found our purpose, we must be smart, efficient, and focus on quality. We are willing to get dirty, dig in, and become masters of artful mistake making as we learn every step of the way. We work with determination, persistence, and pride throughout.

We all have to work hard—no matter who we are or what kind of wild work we're doing. Consider Laird Hamilton, spectacular images of him ripping down giant waves grace the cover of magazines, captivating and inspiring people globally. But the magazines don't show what's going on backstage. Wildpreneurs know that he's taken many knocks to get to those bliss moments and cover shots. When he crashes, he crashes *hard*. It takes commitment, focus, and work every single day, not to mention tremendous patience and perseverance (and maybe a little bit of craziness!) to get back on the board and keep trying.[71]

If we are wise, we choose work that we're willing to put extra effort into—that's when we know we're on the right track. "This is the most simple and basic component of life: Our struggles determine our successes. So, choose your struggles wisely," says Mark Manson.[72] When it comes to the work we're doing, we get to pick our problems (to some extent). We must ask, "What kicks us in the ass in a good way?" For many of us, surfing is a great example—if we come out of the water from surfing, grinning and saying, "That was hard!" and yet eager to go back out there and get our asses kicked once again, then we know we've found something worth working for. Alternatively, if we come out of the water cursing the board bitterly, the work will feel much harder, and we will be much less likely to stick with it in the long run.

Thus, we choose our work wisely. Our work as Wildpreneurs is hard, but our most difficult work moments may also spark our most powerful inspiration.

PRINCIPLE #4—THE POWER OF PLAY

We make play a priority. Whether it's running on a long beach, sailing, dominoes with our amigos, or salsa dancing, we must find playtime that allows us to lose track of time and surrender to joy. There is a sacred power to play[73] that keeps the channels of inspiration flowing. (I get my best ideas while trail running and surfing. What about you? What sparks your best ideas?). Nothing lights up the brain like play.[74]

The reasons to play are countless. Play has the transformative ability to reconnect us with our inner child—a reminder to live in the present, be awed by the wonders around us, and to approach the world with a beginner's mind. Zen teacher Shunryu Suzuki explains that, "In the beginner's mind there are many possibilities; in the expert's mind, there are few." As we excel professionally and become masters of our trades, we stay connected with our playful inner child. *New York Times* writer Karen Rinaldi writes about her experience as a beginner surfer:

> I suck at it. In the sport of (Hawaiian) kings, I'm a jester. In surfing parlance, a "kook." I fall and flail. I get hit on the head by my own board . . . When I do catch a wave, I'm rarely graceful. Once, I actually cried tears of joy over what any observer would have thought a so-so performance on a so-so wave. Yes, I was moved to tears by mediocrity. So why continue? Why pursue something I'll never be good at? Because it's great to suck at something. By taking off the pressure of having to excel at or master an activity, we allow ourselves to live in the moment. You might think this sounds simple enough, but living in the present is also something most of us suck at.[75]

Play can also make us smarter; we cultivate a plethora of useful qualities while frolicking. For example, learning a new sport can teach us humility, patience, perseverance, problem solving, team work (depending on the sport), presence (complete focus on the task at hand), and more. It can also help us to manage stress: the good stress from play (i.e., getting knocked around by the waves while learning to surf) has the power to heal any bad stress that may come with running our own businesses. Play is also key to preventing burn out and keeps us from getting "stuck."

Go play—that's an order not an option—to keep the waves of inspiration coming.

PRINCIPLE #5—
GETTING SLOW, CONSCIOUS LIVING

To complement our lifestyle of awesomeness, action, and steady progress, Wildpreneurs know the importance of getting slow. Let the hare sprint on by as you reconnect with your inner tortoise. Giving pause allows the inspiration we're chasing to catch up with us! Our ability to pause and go deep within ourselves—to sit quietly alone—is essential for reconnecting with our intuition, creativity, and wisdom. Retreating regularly within—momentarily letting go of productivity, shutting down our busy brains and tuning into our hearts—is essential for balance. If our lives are too full and too fast—when we take out the natural spaces, the gaps, the pauses, and the silence—we lose our ability to regenerate and recharge and leave no room for inspiration to find us. We must take time to linger longer.[76] *Slow down and everything you are chasing will finally catch up with you.*[77]

What's the rush anyhow? "The trouble with life in the fast lane is that you get to the other end in an awful hurry," points out soccer player John Jensen. Living faster doesn't make us any better or smarter. In fact, the faster we move, the less carefully we reflect on things. Being smart does not necessarily equate to being wise.[78] Don't be fooled—smartphones (time-saving devices?) won't make us wise. Our "growing reliance on technology is conspiring to create a noisy traffic jam between us and our place of insight and peace," says Huffington.

Slowing down is also an opportunity for a rich journey inward. We definitely don't want to miss out on this aspect of the adventure! Much inspiration resides within, but we must look deep to discover it. "Ideas are like fish, if you want to catch little fish, you can stay in the shallow water. But if you want to catch the big fish, you've got to go deeper. Down deep, the fish are more powerful and more pure," says David Lynch, meditator and author of *Catching the Big Fish*. Going deep may also bring us our treasure.

Why is slowing down so hard? Time is a tricky thing made even more complex by minds that are exhilarated by drama, action, adrenaline, and excitement. Though getting slow may seem dull in comparison, it is the key to finding enduring inspiration (not just quick fixes). Slowing down may be uncomfortable at first, but eventually, we will discover that life isn't about chasing the seconds, it's about fully living them. Slowing down is actually a bit like waking up. Oprah explains: "The whole point of being alive is to become the person you were intended to be, to grow out of and into yourself again and again. I believe you can do this only when you stop long enough to hear the whisper you might have drowned out, the small voice compelling you toward your calling."

As we practice the art of slowing down, we may look to other animals for inspiration—they instinctively know that stopping and slowing down are the best ways to heal themselves. The cheetah—the fastest land animal on Earth—spends up to eighteen hours a day sleeping, but it can accelerate from zero to sixty miles per hour in just three seconds. "They're sleeping their way to the top of the animal kingdom," says Huffington. Einstein also slept for ten hours every night and reportedly stared out his window at the elm trees on the Princeton campus for two hours a day as a way to get beyond the busy mind.

May we channel the wisdom of the cheetah and Einstein as we get slow; unplug and trade busy for lives full of inspiration. So, go ahead, sit back, and join the Mexican fisherman in the hammock zone—no stresspassing!

PRINCIPLE #6—LAUGHTER MEDICINE
Jungle Judi's favorite joke:

> Husband is lying in the hammock. Wife comes up to him and asks, "What are you doing?"

"Nothing," he responds.

"You did that all day yesterday," she says.

"Yeah, and I wasn't finished!" he exclaims.

Wildpreneurship is a comedy. If we can't laugh at the ridiculousness of it all, our inspiration will certainly fizzle. In the jungle, we've lead kayak tours and forgotten all 16 kayak paddles at home. We've had a guest inadvertently get locked in a bedroom for so long that he had to dismantle the door handle with a bottle opener (and plenty of beer for support). We've had soggy yogis covered in mud trying to get their car unstuck on the jungle road in a storm. We've had *tejones* (jungle monkeys) eat all of the chef's organic superfoods and steal a bag of dirty underwear from a guest's casita! Oops. What can ya do? The embarrassing, yet hilarious moments will no doubt continue. Too much serious is a bummer. Why bother? Keep it light—we've gotta laugh to stay sane.

Life is funny, let's laugh at it together. Laughter is good medicine. Giggles will keep the inspiration flowing.

PRINCIPLE #7—TOGETHER

Support is the golden key to the door of inspiration and success. The energy around us—friends, mentors, fellow business owners, community, pets, plants, whatever works for you—should be positive. We surround ourselves with a community of Wildpreneurs and other inspired souls who believe in us and themselves. Hope, optimism, love, and positivity drive the wheel of inspiration, not to mention keep us steady through the turbulence of wild business. We may perpetuate this cycle by both giving and receiving emotional support. We have one mouth and two ears—listen to others twice as much as we speak. Care and empathy are miracle workers. May we revel in the richness and beauty of the journey together.

As we support one another, why not synergize as well? Our work as individuals is exponentially more powerful if we unite—our tiny individual ripples will merge to create powerful waves of inspiration that may create a sea change in our communities. We have the opportunity to spread the good and love of holistic business throughout the world.

POWER POSE

Give yourself a boost of support anytime with a power pose. Stand strong and tall with your arms stretched high above your head, like superman ready to fly—don't you feel empowered? Healthy posture and power poses are essential for walking the talk of support. How we carry ourselves throughout the day affects the energy that we project, and consequently, our inter-actions with others. Slumped shoulders are no way to go through the day.

✳   ✳   ✳

With support in many forms, the inspiration will flow and we will have the strength and courage to embrace inevitable change, transition, and whatever comes next. We will boldly reach for the next trapeze bar of life.

Sometimes, I feel that my life is a series of trapeze swings. I'm either hanging on to a trapeze bar swinging along or, for a few moments, I'm hurdling across space between the trapeze bars. Each time I am afraid I will miss, that I will be crushed on unseen rocks in the bottomless basin between the bars. But I do it anyway. I must. It can be terrifying. It can also be enlightening. Hurtling through the void, we just may learn to fly.

—DANAAN PARRY, AUTHOR
OF *WARRIORS OF THE HEART*[79]

WHERE THE WIND BLOWS

Over the last decade, the Tailwind Jungle Lodge has found its wings. Inspiration has guided us through headwinds of challenge and blissful tailwinds. As we continue to work happily in the wilds of the jungle, my thoughts often drift back to the morning of El Tigre's birthday on the Baja in 2007. I wrote the following in my journal that day:

> The Baja dawn illuminated a mysterious wall of fog on the horizon. As we launched our kayaks, we were enveloped in clouds, a thin shroud of mist at first, then a fog so dense that we were forced to land at the nearest beach, fearful that we would be lost at sea. With nothing to do but wait, Rhett, Tigre, and I drifted into a collective siesta. We awoke to find that the fog lifted, unveiling surroundings that stunned us into silence: PARADISE.

Wildpreneurs navigate our way through the storms and the fog, but when the skies do clear (and you know they will), we will discover our paradise—a place where inspiration flows freely, the beauty of the moment is exquisite and dreams become reality.

Many more paradises and wildness await. What's on the horizon for you, fellow Wildpreneur? **What footprints will you leave on this Earth?** What holistic business will you create? What synergies do you seek?

My next step? Here in the jungle, my Tarzan is teaching me to sail. As we learn to capture the natural power of the wind together, the possibilities for our journey have broadened. Though a tropical tailwind at our backs will always be cherished, we are now equipped to harness and ride winds from all directions—headwinds, crosswinds, and beyond. Where will the wind blow us next?

Smile. Enjoy the ride. Let's get wild!

With love,
TAMARA JACOBI,
AKA "THE JUNGLE GIRL"

ACKNOWLEDGMENTS

Wildpreneurs blew in on the same breeze of inspiration that created my wild business in the jungle. Infinite gracias to Mother Nature for teaching me to go with the flow and to my jungle family—El Tigre (papa Jacobi), Jungle Judi (mama Jacobi), and my Tarzan (Walter Wright) for picking me up, dusting me off, and making me stronger while our sandy labs Pancho, Paris, and Coco gave me countless kisses. Cheers to my brothers, Rhett and Jarrod, for challenging, pushing, and putting up with me. May our life adventures continue! Love to my jungle baby (coming to life at the same time as this book!). The creative inspiration and life force are flowing through mind and body.

Coastal gusts blow me into the tropical community of San Pancho, where the spirit of Wildpreneurship inspires me on every corner. My local support system—Britta Jankay, Tom Robison, Cori Jacobs, Shannon Hughes, Javier Chavez, Mary Bolton, Shanti Tilling, Kelly Guenther, Dakota Bellicci, Natacha Radojevic, Nicole Swedlow, Toto Flores, Gisela Marin, and so many others—thank you for TODO! It was in San Pancho that the tribe of Wildpreneurs began and continues to grow. Gracias to my free-spirited interviewees globally for sharing your wild wisdom in this book.

As the tropical winds shift each spring, the lodge goes into hibernation and my Tarzan, Paris, and I migrate north to our home in the Colorado Rockies where crisp air, columbines, bluegrass, 14ers, and

Wildpreneurs are gloriously plentiful. Many thanks to my Ridgway/ Telluride amigos for cheering me on: Jack Sherman, Kerstin May, Ashley Slater, Casey Day, and Brian Scranton. My vision of holistic businesses was fueled by the majestic San Juan Mountains and enhanced by annual ski trips to Rossland, in the Kootenay Mountains of British Columbia. Paul Girardi and Danielle Hachey: Your hearts, cabin, community, and secret powder stashes are *awesome*.

Midsummer, a west wind blows us to Lake George and the New York Adirondacks where the Wright family opens their lovely home to us. Bald eagles and loons keep me company on swims that sparked countless ideas for this book. Mahalo Nancy, Forrest, Joel, Becca, Eaden, Elsa, Mabel Wright, and the Silver Bay community for your unwavering encouragement.

A zephyr guides me back to my alma mater, Middlebury College, Vermont, where the encouragement of Carolyn Barnwell, Becky Cushing, Zoey Burrows, Elissa Denton, Julia McKinnon, Megan Michelson, and John Kruchoski made all the difference as I hatched my original business plan. Special thanks for support from Bill McKibben, Don Mitchell, and my classmates at 350.org.

When the wind turns cooler, we ride the currents of red maple leaves north to Lake Memphremagog, Quebec, where I grew up. Merci to my Cedarville friends (Yves, Toto, Lynne, Beattie, Safdie, Anders, Montgomery, Setlakwe, and Langlois families) for guiding my young mind in a free-spirited direction. The annual hoopla of Canadian turkey day fills our tummies and hearts before the long migration back to the jungle each October.

My extended writing process was guided by the sharp mind and expertise of writing coach Herta Feely while my brilliant accountability buddy and naturopath, Dr. Kendall Hassemer, kept me on track with her tireless listening and support. And, of course, a grand finale thanks to Tim Burgard, Sicily Axton, Hiram Centeno, and the Harper-Collins Leadership team for giving my book and the voice of Wildpreneurs wings to ride Tailwinds far and wide.

DIRECTORY
OF INTERVIEWEES

Alex Perazasato and Flor Felix Medina:
Nectar Health @nectarhealthyfoods

Alondra Maldonado:
Sabores de Nayarit, saboresdenayarit.com @sabores_de_nayarit

Anelise and Tyler Salvo:
Tahoe Sailing Charters, tahoesail.com @tahoesailingcharters

Annie Kerr:
Wild Balance Jewelry, thewildbalance.com @wildbalance

Ashley Williams:
Rizzarr, rizzarr.com @rizzarrinc

Carolina Daza and Francesca Lo Cascio:
Yala Collective, YALAcreativelab.com @yalacollective

Carolyn Barnwell:
carolynbarnwell.com @carolyn_barnwell

Casey Day:
Powder Factory Skis, powderfactory.com @powderfactoryskis

Cayla Marvil:
Lamplighter Brewery, lamplighterbrewing.com @lamplighterbrew

Cori Jacobs:
Cori Jacobs Gallery, corijacobsgallery.com @corijacobsgallery

Dan Abrams:
Flylow, flylowgear.com @flylowgear

Darrin Polischuk:
Evolove Media, evolovemedia.com @evolovemedia

Derek Loudermilk:
The Art of Adventure, derekloudermilk.com @artofadventurepodcast

Donnie Rust:
The Lost Executive, thelostexecutive.com @thelostexecutive

Drew Cappabianca:
The Hub, thehubadk.com @thehubadk

Emily King:
WheresMyOfficeNow, wheresmyofficenow.com @wheresmyofficenow

Jaime Acosta:
Punta Monterrey Resort, monterreybeach.com @puntamonterrey

Javier Chavez:
Wildmex Surf, wildmex.com @wildmexadventure

Jen Hinton:
Carve Designs, carvedesigns.com @carvedesigns

Jen McCarthy:
BluHouse Market & Café, bluhousecafe.com @bluhousecafe

Jordan Duvall:
IgniteYourSoulBrand, jordanduvall.com @igniteyoursoulbrand

Jungle Judi:
Tailwind Jungle Lodge, tailwindjunglelodge.com
@tailwindjunglelodge

Katie and Spencer Graves:
Eatery 66, eatery66.com @eatery66

Katie Visco:
Katievisco.com @katievisco

Karen Rinaldi:
krinaldi.com @suckatsomething

Dr. Kendall Hassemer:
Naturopathic Dr., drkendallhassemer.com @kendallhassemer

Liz Clark:
Swell Captain, swellvoyage.com @captainlizclark

Mandy Burstein:
Mandyburnstein.com @zengirlmandy

Megan Michelson:
meganmichelson.com & tahoemill.com @meganmichelson

Megan Taylor Morrison:
megantaylormorrison.com @megantaylormorrison

Melissa Goodwin:
Girl Gotta Hike, girlgottahike.com @girlgottahike

Mike Rosenberg:
Garuka Energy Bars, garukabars.com @garukabars

Mike Wood:
SuSalmon, susalmonco.com @susalmonco

Natacha Radojevic:
Moana Surf Adventures, moanasurflife.com @oceanismyoffice

Nick Polinko:
Rumpl, rumpl.com @gorumpl

Nicolas Blevins:
Acupuncture, @nicooaventuras

Nicole Swedlow:
EntreAmigos, entreamigos.org.mx @entreamigos_sanpancho

Paul Girardi and Danielle Hachey:
Feathers & Fur Retreats, feathersandfur.ca @feathersfur

Peter Hall:
Hala SUP Boards, halagear.com @halagearsup

Rhett Jacobi:
Arbor Construction, arborconstruction.com @dirt_road_development

Rick Kahn:
rdkahn.com

Sarah Love:
I Stand For Love, istandforlove.com @istandforlove

Shannon Hughes:
Pancho Vida & TerraMar Realty, terramarrealty.com @shannonh1111

Shanti Tilling:
SweatPlayLive, sweatplaylive.com @sweatplaylive

Shelby Stanger:
Wild Ideas Worth Living, wildideasworthliving.com @wildideasworthliving

Shep and Ian Murray
Vineyard Vines, vineyardvines.com @vineyardvines

Stephanie Gauvin:
Artist, artiststephaniegauvin.com @stephaniegauvinartist

Susan Horning and Nicola Bennett:
Unity Yoga, www.unityyoga.ca @unityyogateahouse

Talia Pollock:
PartyInMyPlants, partyinmyplants.com @partyinmyplants

Tamara Jacobi:
Tailwind Jungle Lodge, tailwindjunglelodge.com @tailwindjunglelodge and Wildpreneurs, wildpreneurs.com @wildpreneurs

Tara Gimmer:
Tara Gimmer Headshots, taragimmerheadshots.com

Theresa Roth:
SuperLoveTees, superlovetees.com @superlovetees

Toto Flores:
Mexicolate, mexicolate.mx @mexicolate

Vitina Blumenthal:
Wanderfulsoul, Wanderwell, Soul Compass, Creative Minds, wanderfulsoul.com, wanderwell.life, soulcompass.life, aligncreativeminds.com @wanderfulsoul

Wally Walsh:
Cerveceria San Pancho, cerveceriaartesanalsanpancho.com @cerverceriaartesanalsanpancho

Yael Flusberg:
yaelflusberg.com @yaelflusberg

ENDNOTES

1. This quotation is from chapter 64 of the *Tao Te Ching*, attributed to Laozi, Chinese philosopher (604–531 BC).
2. Pema Chödrön, *When Things Fall Apart: Heart Advice for Difficult Times* (Boston, MA: Shambhala Publications, 2000).
3. Justin Bariso, "Why Entrepreneurs Don't Need a College Degree," June 24, 2015, *Inc.* Accessed at https://www.inc.com/justin-bariso/why-entrepreneurs-don-t-need-a-college-degree.html.
4. Marianne Williamson, *A Return to Love: Reflections on the Principles of A COURSE IN MIRACLES* (New York: HarperCollins, 2009).
5. Tim Ferriss, *The Tim Ferriss Show,* podcast episode #249, "How to Make a Difference and Find Your Purpose." Accessed at https://www.stitcher.com/podcast/the-tim-ferriss-show/e/50613732.
6. Chrissie Wellington, *A Life Without Limits: A World Champion's Journey* (New York: Center Street, 2012, 2013).
7. John Mackey, *Conscious Capitalism* (Boston, MA: Harvard Business Review Press, 2014).
8. Henry David Thoreau, *Walden* (New York: George Routledge & Sons, 1904), p. 46.
9. Adam Grant, *Originals* (London: W H Allen, 2017).
10. R. A. Montgomery, *Choose Your Own Adventure* (Waitsfield, VT: Chooseco, 2005).
11. Jillian D'Onfro, "9 successful entrepreneurs share their best career advice," *Business Insider*, January 26, 2016. Accessed at: https://www.businessinsider.com/advice-and-tips-from-entrepreneurs-2016-1.

12. Brendon Burchard, *High Performance Habits: How Extraordinary People Become That Way* (Carlsbad, CA: Hay House, 2017).
13. Grant, *Originals.*
14. Burchard, *High Performance Habits.*
15. Tim Grahl, *Your First 1000 Copies: The Step-by-Step Guide to Marketing Your Book.* (Lynchburg, VA: Out:think Group, 2013).
16. Derek Loudermilk, *Superconductors: Revolutionize Your Career and Make Big Things Happen* (London: Kogan Page, Ltd., 2018), p. 117.
17. Sustainable Travel International. Accessed at http://sustainabletravel.org/.
18. Google, "Discover How to Use Google Ads to Reach Your Goals." Accessed at https://adwords.google.com/home/how-it-works/.
19. A. J. Jacobs, "How Does a Year of Following Biblical Rules Change You?" TED Radio Hour, August 14, 2015, National Public Radio. Accessed at https://www.npr.org/programs/ted-radio-hour/431363633/amateur-hour.
20. https://sites.hks.harvard.edu/m-rcbg/papers/michael_michael_march_07.pdf.
21. Elisa Batista, "Thriving After Transitioning to a Third Metric Life," *The Huffington Post.* May 21, 2014. Accessed at https://www.huffingtonpost.com/elisa-batista/thriving-after-transitioning-to-a-third-metric-life_b_5359269.html.
22. Ferriss, "Introduction—My Story," *The Tim Ferriss Show* (blog). Accessed at https://www.stitcher.com/podcast/the-tim-ferriss-show/e/50613732.
23. Greg McKeown, *Essentialism: The Disciplined Pursuit of Less* (London: Virgin Books, 2014).
24. Linda Stone, "Continuous Partial Attention," February 7, 2011. Accessed at https://lindastone.net/qa/continuous-partial-attention/.
25. Arianna Huffington, *Thrive: The Third Metric to Redefining Success and Creating a Life of Well-being, Wisdom, and Wonder* (New York: Baker & Taylor, 2015).
26. Liz Clark, "Staying True to You: Staying Afloat Financially." Swell Voyage. January 10, 2017. Accessed at https://swellvoyage.com/2017/01/staying-true-to-you-staying-afloat-financially/.
27. Janine M. Benyus, *Biomimicry* (New York: Morrow, 1998).
28. Biomimicry Institute. "DesignLens: Life's Principles." Accessed at https://biomimicry.net/the-buzz/resources/designlens-lifes-principles/.
29. For more information about Entreamigos, go to www.entreamigos.org.mx.

30. Jack C. Smith, *God and Mr. Gomez* (Santa Barbara, CA: Capra Press, 1997).

31. Mark Manson, *The Subtle Art of Not Giving a F*ck: A Counterintuitive Approach to Living a Good Life (New York: Harper, 2016).*

32. Kyle Kowalski, "'Then What?' The Story of the Tourist and the Fisherman." Sloww (blog), June 4, 2017. Accessed at https://www.sloww.co /tourist-fisherman/. This story is also adapted and told by Courtney Carver in *Soulful Simplicity* and Timothy Ferriss in *The 4-Hour Work Week.*

33. Jack Kerouac, *On the Road.* (New York: Penguin Books, 2018).

34. Buddha Quotes. BrainyQuote.com, BrainyMedia Inc, 2018. Accessed at https://www.brainyquote.com/quotes/buddha_164946.

35. Huffington, *Thrive.*

36. Oscar Wilde Quotes. BrainyQuote.com, BrainyMedia Inc, 2018. Accessed at https://www.brainyquote.com/quotes/oscar_wilde_103614.

37. Shanti Tilling, "Scar—A Love Story," Sweat Play Live, November 15, 2016. Accessed at https://sweatplaylive.com/mindset/scar-a-love-story/.

38. Maria Popova, "There Is a Crack in Everything, That's How the Light Gets In: Leonard Cohen on Democracy and Its Redemptions" Brain Pickings. December 20, 2016. Accessed at https://www.brainpickings .org/2016/11/10/leonard-cohen-democracy/.

39. Joshua Rosenthal, *Integrative Nutrition: Feed Your Hunger for Health & Happiness* (New York: Institute for Integrative Nutrition, 2014).

40. Rosenthal, *Integrative Nutrition.*

41. Rosenthal, *Integrative Nutrition.*

42. Michael Pollan, *The Omnivore's Dilemma* (New York: The Penguin Press, 2007).

43. Alexandra Jamieson, *Women, Food, and Desire: Embrace Your Cravings, Make Peace with Your Food, Reclaim Your Body* (New York: Gallery Books, 2016).

44. Stuart Brown, "Play is more than just fun." TED, 2008. Accessed at https://www.ted.com/talks/stuart_brown_says_play_is_more_than_fun _it_s_vital/transcript#t-142000.

45. John C. Maxwell Quotes. BrainyQuote.com, BrainyMedia Inc, 2018. Accessed at https://www.brainyquote.com/quotes/john_c_maxwell _600892.

46. Aimee Groth, "Sheryl Sandberg: 'The Most Important Career Choice You'll Make Is Who You Marry,'" *Business Insider Australia.* December 1, 2011. Accessed at https://www.businessinsider.com.au/sheryl-sandberg -career-advice-to-women-2011-12.

47. Edgar Rice Burroughs, *Tarzan of the Apes* (Chicago, IL: A. C. Mc-Clurg, 1912).

48. *Dear Sugar Radio* is an "advice column" podcast hosted by Cheryl Strayed and Steve Almond on National Public Radio. Accessed at https://www.npr.org/podcasts/469249288/dear-sugar-radio.

49. *Tapatío*—A Mexican from Guadalajara. *Chilango*—A Mexican from Mexico City.

50. Air Force Special Operations Command's pararescuemen, also known as PJs, belong to an elite force trained and equipped to conduct conventional and unconventional rescue operations.

51. Marianne Williamson, *A Return to Love: Reflections on the Principles of A COURSE IN MIRACLES* (New York: HarperOne, 1996).

52. Esther Perel, "The secret to desire in a long-term relationship," TED, February 2013. Accessed at https://www.ted.com/talks/esther_perel_the_secret_to_desire_in_a_long_term_relationship?source=email.

53. Gary Chapman, *The 5 Love Languages: The Secret to Love that Lasts* (Chicago, IL: Moody Publishers, 2014).

54. Jay Goltz, "How to Be an Entrepreneur, and Stay Married," *The New York Times*, October 1, 2014. Accessed at https://boss.blogs.nytimes.com/2014/10/01/how-to-be-an-entrepreneur-and-stay-married/.

55. Tara Giacobbo, personal communication from Rossland, British Columbia.

56. Bill George, "The Power of Mindful Leadership," *The Huffington Post*, July 27, 2016. Accessed at https://www.huffingtonpost.com/bill-george/the-power-of-mindful-lead_b_7878482.html.

57. Thích Nhất Hạnh, *No Mud, No Lotus: The Art of Transforming Suffering* (Berkeley, CA: Parallax Press, 2014).

58. Chödrön, *When Things Fall Apart.*

59. Huffington, *Thrive.*

60. XPT, "Performance Breathing.®" Accessed at https://www.xptlife.com/performance-breathing/.

61. Dan Harris, *10% Happier: How I Tamed the Voice in My Head, Reduced Stress without Losing My Edge, and Found Self-Help That Actually Works: A True Story* (London: Yellow Kite, 2017).

62. Curby Rule (2001), "The Deeper Meaning of Aloha," Aloha International. Accessed at https://www.huna.org/html/deeper.html.

63. Gary Chapman, *The 5 Love Languages: How to Express Heartfelt Commitment to Your Mate* (Bhopal, India: Manjul Publishing, 2010).

64. This phrase typically appears as "I will not let anyone walk through my mind with their dirty feet" and is often attributed to Mahatma

Gandhi. For more information, see https://ask.metafilter.com/157716 /Help-on-Gandhi-aphorism.

65. Janna Delgado, "Heart Opening through Metta Meditation." Kripalu Center for Yoga and Health. Accessed at https://kripalu.org/resources /heart-opening-through-metta-meditation.

66. Vicki Corona, "Life is not measured by the number of breaths we take, but by the moments that take our breath away." Quote Investigator. Accessed at https://quoteinvestigator.com/2013/12/17/breaths/.

67. Pico Iyer, "Where Is Home?" TED. Accessed at https://www.ted.com /talks/pico_iyer_where_is_home/transcript. Idea from Marcel Proust, French novelist: "The sense of seeing something for the first time, even if you have actually witnessed it many times before."

68. Arianna Huffington, "The Third Metric to Success," Issue 17: July 2014, *Foundr* magazine. Accessed at https://foundr.com/magazine /arianna-huffington-issue-17-july-2014-2/.

69. Clark, "Staying True to You: Staying Afloat Financially."

70. Wellington, *A Life Without Limits*.

71. Karen Rinaldi, "(It's Great to) Suck at Something." *The New York Times*, April 29, 2017. Accessed at https://www.nytimes.com/2017/04 /28/opinion/its-great-to-suck-at-surfing.html.

72. Mark Manson, "The Most Important Question of Your Life," November 6, 2013. Accessed at https://markmanson.net/question.

73. Alexandra Jamieson, "The Power of Play," *Sacred Play* podcast.

74. Brown, "Play is more than just fun," TED, 2008.

75. Rinaldi, "(It's Great to) Suck at Something."

76. Courtney Carver, *Soulful Simplicity: How Living with Less Can Lead to So Much More*. (New York: Tarcherperigee, 2017).

77. "Wise Old Sayings." Curiosity Sayings and Curiosity Quotes. Accessed at http://www.wiseoldsayings.com/slow-down-quotes/.

78. Guy Raz (host), "Slowing Down," TED Radio Hour, August 26, 2016, NPR. Accessed at https://www.npr.org/programs/ted-radio-hour /490624293/slowing-down.

79. Danaan Parry, *Warriors of the Heart* (Kalaheo, HI: Earthstewards Network, 2012).

INDEX

holistic wellness habits (*cont.*)
    nourishment without food, 161–62
    nutrition, 75, 164–65
Holmes, Oliver Wendell, Sr., 81
Horning, Susan, 219–20
The Hub, 33–34
Huffington, Arianna, 106, 155, 205, 211,
    213, 215, 225, 230
Hughes, Shannon, 21, 51, 138, 162

Ignite Your Soul Brand, 18
imagination, 8
INN (Institute for Integrative Nutrition), 75,
    203
inspiration, 221–33
    as "primary food," 161
    principles for, 224–32, *see also* code of
      living
    roadmap for, 221
Institute for Integrative Nutrition (IIN), 75,
    203
intention
    loving, 10, 213–18
    power of, 21
    setting, 22
interest, 18
intuition, 24
investing
    reinvesting income, 60, 67–68
    in yourself, 72, 151–54, *see also* wellness
I Stand for Love, 66, 211–13

Jacobi, Judi "Jungle Judi," 21
    on attitude, 216
    background of, 28–29, 172–74, 176–77
    in creation of Tailwind, 28, 32, 33, 35, 40,
      43–44
    and daughter's love life, 190
    at end of kayaking trip, 23
    favorite joke of, 230–31
    gift from, 185
    and mistakes at Tailwind, 47
    personality of, 183
    on sacredness in revelry, 83, 168
    and Tailwind finances, 56
    at ten-year anniversary, 222
Jacobi, Rhett
    Arbor Construction business of, 60–61
    background of, 11, 173–74, 176–77
    and Baja kayak trip, 1, 2
    as devil's advocate, 11–12
    graduation of, 47
    on pelicans, 131
    on working, 109
Jacobi, Tigre "El Tigre"
    background of, 4, 15, 172–74, 176–77

    and Baja kayak trip, 1–2, 23
    in creation of Tailwind, 28, 32, 33, 35, 39, 40
    daydreaming by, 7, 8
    on eco-lodge business plan, 20–21
    family business vision of, 178
    interview with, 5–6
    on mindset, 132
    and mistakes at Tailwind, 47
    personality of, 183, 184
    on self-doubt, 16
    on simplicity and minimalism, 15–16, 20–21
    and Tailwind finances, 56
    on technology, 10
    at ten-year anniversary, 222
Jacobs, A. J., 103, 142
Jacobs, Cori, 72
Jamieson, Alexandra, 163
Jankay, Britta, 119, 120
Jensen, John, 229
Jobs, Steve, 9
journaling, 104
Jungle Girl Health coaching, 75

Kahn, Rick, 142, 143
kayaking test, 195–97
Kerouac, Jack, 147
Kerr, Annie, 33, 47–48, 67
King, Emily, 52–54
King, Stephen, 76
Koch, Jim, 86

Lamplighter Brewing, 45–46
Laozi, 1
laughter medicine, 230–31
legal requirements, 106
let that sh*t go exercise, 157
The Life & Love of the Sea (Blackwell), 225
Lincoln, Abraham, 43
listening to your body, 163–64
location, 30–32
logo, 94, 98
The Lost Executive magazine, 148–49
Loudermilk, Derek, 87–88, 98
love
    as antidote to drama, 213–18
    for family business, 186
    languages of, 195–97
    as "primary food," 161
    for what you do, 149
    in working through conflict, 10
    see also romantic relationships
Love, Sarah, 66, 211–13
Lynch, David, 229–30

Mackey, John, 62
Maldonado, Alondra, 145–46

FINAL THOUGHTS: GET WILD & LIVE THE GOOD LIFE

Shep & Ian Murray—

Brothers & Cofounders of Vineyard Vines

"We were stuck behind desks in jobs we didn't like . . . and we were miserable. So we quit. We tossed out business suits for bathing suits, got our wisdom teeth pulled while we still had coverage, and signed up for every credit card we could. On the same day, within ten minutes of each other, we walked out of our jobs, grabbed a drink, and started chasing our dream. We had plenty of doors slammed in our faces, but it's like they say: when one door closes, go in through the window."

Advice

If you have a solid dream in whatever industry you want to embark in, pursue it wholeheartedly. We had careers in industries that didn't necessarily reflect what Vineyard Vines is today, however we saw a need and stopped at nothing to create great product for great people. Over twenty years in, though some things have changed, we're still the same at our core—having fun and sharing the gift of the vineyard with everyone we can.

The Good Life

Nearly a year before Vineyard Vines was created, we were on vacation when we found the key to life was enjoying it with the people you love. We wanted to embrace and share this philosophy and lifestyle. During dinner one night, we told a friend that we wanted to find a way for people to bring the "good life" with them every day to work and would do so through whimsical neckties that represented all of the finer places and things in life.

✳   ✳   ✳